Faith Jump
Vol 1.0

T.K. ANDERSON

NIA BOOKS
Scottsdale, Arizona

Published by NIA BOOKS
Scottsdale, Arizona (USA)

In Partnership With:
The Social Media Church (TSMchurch.com)
The National Institute of Apologetics (NIAonline.net)

©2017, T.K. Anderson; *Faith Jump Vol 1.0*

All rights reserved.
No part of this book may be used or reproduced in any manner whatsoever without written permission except in the case of brief quotations embodied in critical articles and reviews.

First edition hardcover: September 2017
First edition eBook: July 2017

ISBN: 978-0-692-91461-8

Printed in the United States of America

Dedication

To those who may find Christ through these writings

and

To those who first helped me in finding Christ —

Pastor's Peterson, Moen, & McDaniel

Along with…

Young Life Leader Dave Allen

II Corinthians 5:17

"Therefore, if anyone is in Christ,

he is a new creation.

The old has passed away;

behold, the new has come."

Contents

Introduction   7

ONE
The Historicity of Jesus   9

TWO
Data Crunching the Resurrection   29

THREE
The Hallucination Theory   53

FOUR
Jesus and Pagan Myths   67

FIVE
Transposition   85

SIX
God's Non-Binding Agreement   95

SEVEN
Is God Alone?   113

EIGHT
What About The Crusades?   129

NINE
Is *Disbelief* in God Reasonable?   145

TEN
The Problem of Evil   169

About the Author   187
Bibliography   189

Introduction

When a person decides to become a follower of Christ, it is usually the type of decision that occurs over an extended period of time. Knowing this, I have set out to provide a set of readings designed to help those who are searching for answers to the toughest questions regarding Jesus Christ. After all, deciding to follow Christ and represent Him on earth is a pronouncement of epic proportions and should not be entered into lightly or superficially. Not that one is prone to do so naturally, however, it is a good reminder that Jesus asked His disciples to count the cost before following Him. *"For which of you, desiring to build a tower, does not first **sit down and count the cost**, whether he has enough to complete it?"* (Luke 14:28).

This volume is geared to provide the reader with solid information, facts, and reasons to support and/or uphold one's belief in Jesus as Savior and Lord. As you read through the chapters, I attempt to provide answers to some of our most perplexing questions regarding God's existence, His interaction with us, and the claims of Jesus and His earliest followers. By design, I spend extra time regarding the most important event in human history, the resurrection of Jesus. Enjoy.

T.K. Anderson, 2017
Pastor, The Social Media Church
TSMchurch.com

T.K. Anderson

CHAPTER ONE
The Historicity of Jesus

You're On The Hook

To be a Christian is to embrace the historicity of Jesus as ascribed to in the Bible. Not only is the Christian committed to the historical aspects of Jesus' life, but he is also on the hook for one of, if not the most incredible event in all of human antiquity, the resurrection of Jesus. In order to arrive at a worldview that embraces miracles such as the resurrection of Jesus, healing of the blind, or divinely inspired authors capturing the events of the Son of God, it would be reasonable to conclude that those who do not hold such a worldview would need first to establish a historical account of the life of Jesus. Hence, the historicity of Jesus becomes an important and necessary first step in the journey of faith in becoming a follower of Jesus.

As to assessing the historical accuracy of the events, those who lived in the region and time of Jesus had a distinct advantage over those of us who now walk the earth some two thousand years later. Even so, in mid-first century A.D., the biblical writer Luke wrote to those alive at the time, *"I myself have carefully investigated everything from the beginning, I too decided to write and orderly account for you, most excellent Theophilus."*[1] From there, he compiled a two-volume account on the life of Jesus. We know these reports today as the Gospel of Luke and the Book of Acts. Similarly, Paul's message of Christian legitimacy is captured in a letter to early Christians in the city of Corinth, *"If Christ has not been raised, our preaching is useless and so is your faith."*[2] We find from these two first-century writers the importance of an essential and necessary confidence in the historical life of Jesus, which leads to certainty in His resurrection from the dead. Even in their time, without such confidence, Luke and Paul concluded Christianity is unworkable.

Knowing History

Yet, we face an even bigger challenge. For those of us in the modern era, "there are numerous challenges to knowing the past."[3] Unfortunately, the past is "forever gone"[4] and in several cases impossible to reconstruct. Dr. Mike Licona writes, "Our knowledge of the past comes exclusively through sources. This

---

[1] Luke 1:3 (NIV), accessed April 12, 2017, http://biblehub.com/luke/1-3.htm.
[2] I Corinthian 15:14 (NIV), accessed April 12, 2017, http://biblehub.com/1_corinthians/15-14.htm.
[3] Michael R. Licona, *The Resurrection of Jesus* (Downers Grove, IL: InterVarsity Press, 2010), 31.
[4] Ibid, 31.

means, to an extent, our only link to the past is through the eyes of someone else, a person who had his or her own opinions and agendas."[5] Because facts of history can be so elusive, the historicity of Jesus is of paramount importance for one to trust in the foundational claims of Christianity, namely the resurrection. I will argue there are three types of historical sources that support confidence in the historicity of Jesus. However, due to the limited size of this chapter, I will keep our discussion of sources to those "that mention the death of Jesus or what happened to him afterward and are thought by at least some scholars to have been written within one hundred years of Jesus."[6]

Extra-Biblical Sources

One of the most compelling reasons in support of the historicity of Jesus is found in the writings of extra-biblical sources. Because I hold this to be one of the most convincing pieces of evidence for skeptics, I will devote the largest portion of the chapter to this section. Simply put, there are no convincing reasons for non-Christian, trustworthy historians to write stories or include pseudo-biographical information regarding fictional persons, including Jesus or otherwise. We have no current credible evidence of authoritative, historical or religious leaders of that period inserting into their texts make-beliefs or mythological figures in place of what we know today to be truly historical figures.

---
[5] Ibid, 31.
[6] Ibid, 201.

Josephus

For one to stretch to the conclusion that Josephus, for example, purposely nullified his historical writings for some nefarious reason carries no weight among Christian or non-Christian scholarship. Licona points out, "Josephus mentions Jesus on two occasions."[7] The first account, however, is not without debate due to a suspecting interpolation by Christian writers "sometime between the first and fourth centuries."[8] The second account, however, does not carry the same concern among scholars. I will start with the second account first.

Account #2

The second account is recorded as, "Convening the judges of the Sanhedrin, he [Ananus] brought before them the brother of Jesus who was called the Christ, whose name was James, and certain others."[9] We have good reason to believe this is an accurate account from Josephus because it "appears in all of the Greek manuscripts of *Antiquities of the Jews 20* without any notable variation."[10] Additionally, New Testament writers continually referred to James in a more reverent way such as the 'brother of the Lord' or 'brother of the Savior.' Josephus, on the other hand, would keep the description to a matter-of-fact format.[11] This leads us to believe there is no tampering of the source by later Christian writers.

---

[7] Ibid, 235.
[8] Ibid, 235.
[9] Ant.20.200 English translation by Maier, P.L. *Josephus: The Essential Works* (Grand Rapids: Kregel, 1994), 281.
[10] Michael R. Licona, *The Resurrection of Jesus* (Downers Grove, IL: InterVarsity Press, 2010), 236.
[11] Ibid, 236.

Lastly, Josephus' reference to Jesus as the one "who was called the Christ" is used in such a way as to distinguish Jesus "from others in his writings by the same name."[12] John Paul Meier points out there are twenty-one different individuals bearing the name *Jesus* in the works of Josephus. He additionally writes, "In fact, the very high priest who succeeded Ananus, who instigated the death of James was Jesus, son of Damnaeus."[13] From this reasoning, we can see why Josephus found it necessary to distinguish Jesus by the title known about him at the time. It is important to remember, Josephus was born in 34 A.D. and therefore was writing his historical accounts well within the time frame of the initial spread of Christianity across his region. I will now transfer in return to the first account.

Account #1

The first account from Josephus is referred to as the *Testimonium Flavianum*. This account has an immense amount of writing regarding interpretation and authenticity arguments. Licona writes, "Scholars hold three general positions on this passage: (1) the entire text is authentic; (2) the entire text is a Christian interpolation; or (3) Josephus mentions Jesus in this text, but it was subsequently doctored by a Christian interpolator. The first two positions have a few adherents; the third enjoys a majority."[14] Of most interest to our discussion is, even if we remove the debated portions of the account, we are left with a

---

[12] Ibid, 237.
[13] John P. Meier, *A Marginal Jew: Rethinking the Historical Jesus. Vol. 2* (New York, NY: Doubleday, 1994), 285.
[14] Michael R. Licona, *The Resurrection of Jesus* (Downers Grove, IL: InterVarsity Press, 2010), 238.

description of Jesus from Josephus that is in overall agreement with the biblical description. With the suspected interpolation portions removed, we read Josephus' account as,

> *At that time there appeared Jesus, a wise man. For he was a doer of startling deeds, a teacher of people who received the truth with pleasure. And he gained a following both among many Jews and among many of Greek origin. And when Pilate, because of an accusation made by the leading men among us, condemned him to the cross, those who had loved him previously did not cease to do so. And up until this very day the tribe of Christians (named after him) has not died out.*[15]

Scholars such as Licona, Meier, Feldman, Allison, Morton Smith, and Zvi Baras all conclude this portion, or the majority of it, is authentic and can be considered valid for historical purposes. Meier resolves this passage coheres well "with Josephus' style and language; the same cannot be said when the text's vocabulary and grammar are compared with that of the NT…In fact, most of the vocabulary turns out to be characteristic of Josephus."[16]

Early Jewish Burial Accounts

As fascinating as this is, Craig Evans argues there are secondary evidences from Jewish writers regarding the burial account of Jesus as found in the Gospels. Evans writes, "Jewish writers…such as Philo and Josephus, indicate that Roman officials

---

[15] John P. Meier, *A Marginal Jew: Rethinking the Historical Jesus. Vol. 1* (New York, NY: Doubleday, 1991), 61.
[16] Ibid, 62-63.

permitted executed Jews to be buried before nightfall."[17] Although Jesus is not mentioned specifically, Evans observes, "Only in times of rebellion...were bodies not taken down from crosses or gibbets and given proper burial."[18]

It is of interest to note that Josephus and Philo's historical accounts match the writings of early Christian authors. Evans holds that this gives additional historical value in discovering an accurate account of the historical Jesus. Because of this consistency and the matters cited above, we are therefore within reason to count both of Josephus' accounts as meaningful in our discussion of the historicity of Jesus.

Additional Writers

Other extra-biblical sources mentioning Jesus include Tacitus, Pliny the Younger, and Suetonius. Tacitus (ca. A.D. 56-120) "is generally regarded as the greatest of the Roman historians."[19] Tacitus mentions Jesus once in his *Annals* written ca. A.D. 116-117. He writes regarding Nero's responsibility for the burning of Rome,

> *Therefore, to squelch the rumor, Nero created scapegoats and subjected to the most refined tortures those whom the common people called "Christians," [a group] hated for their abominable crimes. Their name comes from Christ, who, during the reign of Tiberius, had been executed by the procurator Pontius Pilate. Suppressed for the moment,*

---

[17] Craig A. Evans, *Jewish Burial Traditions and the Resurrection of Jesus* (Thousand Oaks, CA: Journal for the Study of the Historical Jesus, 2005), Vol. 3.2, 233.
[18] Ibid, 233.
[19] M.T. Gilderhus, *History and Historians: A Historiographical Introduction*. 6th ed. (Upper Saddle River, N.J.: Prentice Hall, 2007), 20.

> *the deadly superstition broke out again, not only in Judea, that land which originated this evil, but also in the city of Rome.*[20]

It is evident from this historical account Tacitus is in agreement with the biblical account of Jesus as the founder of Christianity in the region of Judea. We find additional biblical agreement with the spread of Christianity across the Roman Empire by 64 A.D., and the execution of Jesus by the edict of Pontius Pilate. Licona points out, "Although the authenticity of this text is occasionally questioned, the vast majority of scholars grant it."[21] The text belongs to the style and language of Tacitus, and there are no credible objections to prove falsity of this account.

Pliny the Younger as a senator and "avid letter writer"[22] wrote to Emperor Trajan near 111 A.D. and included information of interest to the formation of early Christianity. Although he does not include any specific language regarding Jesus' death or resurrection, we are able to utilize his writings as corroborating evidence relating to the life of Jesus in general. Admittedly, this historical account is not as descriptive as the former two, but yet it can serve to show a broader scope regarding additional historians having knowledge of Jesus.

Likewise, Suetonius a "lawyer and Roman historian"[23] composed biographies of Caesars (Julius Caesar through

---

[20] Tacitus *Ann.* 15.44 English translations by Meier (1991), 89-90.
[21] Michael R. Licona, *The Resurrection of Jesus* (Downers Grove, IL: InterVarsity Press, 2010), 243.
[22] Ibid, 244.
[23] Ibid, 244.

Domitian) between A.D. 117 and 122. In one of those biographies, he includes an event that was also captured by Luke in Acts 18:2, "Claudius had ordered all Jews to leave Rome."[24] Suetonius, similar to Luke, writes, "He [Claudius] expelled the Jews from Rome, since they were always making disturbances because of the instigator Chrestus."[25] There is some debate as to who "Chrestus" is, but scholars do maintain and "generally believe that this event occurred in A.D. 49"[26] as recorded by Luke in the book of Acts. The similarities of Acts and this text are too evident to ignore the clear relationship of "Chrestus" as a highly probable reference to Jesus.

Therefore, one can conclude this text weighs heavily in favor of our thesis. Through the writings of these four non-Christian historians, we find a common theme regarding the person of Jesus and His fate. Additionally, there is a general scholarly agreement on what was "in the air"[27] at the time within the minds of these and other pagan writers such as Mara bar Serapion, Thallus, Lucian, and Celsus. The evidence firmly points to the fact that the biblical Jesus existed and did so in a way that is supported by non-Christian sources, which of great interest are also compatible with Christian sources. It seems to me, based upon this one line of reasoning alone that, the historicity of Jesus can be generally established. However, I wish to present a second line of reasoning in support of a positive case for the historicity of Jesus.

---

[24] Acts 18:2 (NIV), accessed April 17, 2017, http://biblehub.com/acts/18-2.htm.
[25] Michael R. Licona, *The Resurrection of Jesus* (Downers Grove, IL: InterVarsity Press, 2010), 244.
[26] Ibid, 244.
[27] Ibid, 246.

The Gospel Accounts

A secondary reason in support of the historicity of Jesus is found in the independent sources of the Gospel accounts. Positive Christian scholarship weighs heavily in favor of utilizing the independent sources of Matthew, Mark, Luke, and John, while non-Christian scholarship takes an opposing view. Patterson writes, "Historical critical scholars of the Bible have maintained for more than a century that the gospels are not history, and in fact were never intended to be read as such."[28] While Keener holds, "[T]he basic portrayal of Jesus in the first-century Gospels, dependent on eyewitnesses, is more plausible than the alternative hypotheses of its modern detractors.... On the whole there is much that we can know about Jesus historically."[29] The question becomes, do the Gospel accounts have validity in the search for the historical Jesus?

Types of Genre

Licona weighs in on this debate by writing, "Prior to the 1990s a large segment of New Testament scholarship maintained that the Gospels represent a *sui generis*, that is, a genre unique to them."[30] This type of genre is mostly viewed as a "type of mythology."[31] Furthermore, according to the Jesus Seminar in 1992, "The gospels are now assumed to be narrative in which the

---

[28] Stephen J. Patterson, *The God of Jesus: The Historical Jesus and the Search for Meaning* (Harrisburg, PA: Trinity Press International, 1998), 214.
[29] Craig S. Keener, *The Historical Jesus of the Gospels* (Grand Rapids, MI: Eerdmans, 2009), 349.
[30] Michael R. Licona, *The Resurrection of Jesus* (Downers Grove, IL: InterVarsity Press, 2010), 201.
[31] Ibid, 201.

memory of Jesus is embellished by mythic elements.... anyone making a claim of historicity pertaining to any portion of them bears the burden of proof."[32] Licona responds, "This question [of what type of genre] has received much attention over the past twenty years, resulting in advances in our understanding of the issue."[33] Licona continues by saying, "As a result, the consensus of scholarship has shifted significantly from the opinion held by the Jesus Seminar."[34]

In support of this claim, Licona cites R.T. France's 2002 work, which concludes,

> *Fifty years ago we were drilled in the critical orthodoxy of the form-critical school which insisted that the Gospels were not to be seen as biographies, but since then there has been a massive swing in scholarly opinion on this point, and increasingly sophisticated study of the nature of biographical writing in the ancient world has led to a general recognition that, for all the distinctiveness of its Christian content and orientation, in terms of literary form Mark's book (and those of Matthew, Luke and John) would have seemed to an educated reader in the first century to fall into roughly the same category as the lives of famous men pioneered by Cornelius Nepos and soon to reach their most famous expression in the 'Parallel Lives' of Plutarch.*[35]

The Change

This recent change in understanding the Gospels as biographical accounts began by the works of Talbert and Burridge.

---

[32] Ibid, 201.
[33] Ibid, 202.
[34] Ibid, 202.
[35] Richard T. France, *The Gospel of Mark* New International Greek Text Commentary (Grand Rapids, MI: Eerdmans, 2002), 5.

Of interest is the fact Burridge set out initially to disprove Talbert's biographical thesis, but during his research on the subject, "[Burridge] reversed his opinion."[36] Burridge discovered the first-century writers were ultimately concerned with the facts of Jesus' life; meaning his birth, ministry, philosophy, death, and resurrection in the same fashion as other Greco-Roman historians and biographers of that period. To treat the Gospel writers differently would be to insert an additional bias against the biblical authors.

David Aune concludes, "Thus while the Evangelists clearly had an important theological agenda, the very fact that they chose to adapt Greco-Roman biographical conventions to tell the story of Jesus indicated that they were centrally concerned to communicate what they thought really happened."[37] We do know that many ancient biographers took liberties when writing about their subjects. However, there is no good reason to accuse the Gospel writers as inscribing fictional or purely mythical accounts especially when their data matches the archaeological, literary, and other evidence of their day.

Divine Inspiration

Lastly, in using the Gospel accounts for establishing the historicity of Jesus, one is free to remove from the debate the argument from divine inspiration. At this point, we are only

---

[36] Michael R. Licona, *The Resurrection of Jesus* (Downers Grove, IL: InterVarsity Press, 2010), 202.
[37] D.E. Aune, *Greco-Roman Literature and the New Testament: Selected Forms and Genres* (Atlanta, GA: Scholars Press, 1998), 125.

arguing from a historical perspective. In other words, did the events purported to have occurred in the Gospel accounts occur, or did they occur in a manner in which those present at the time believed those events to have occurred? We are not arguing for miracles to be real at this point, we are only establishing the person and historicity of Jesus according to the biographies of His day. Later in our study, we are then able to dissect the concepts of supernatural intervention and answer the question; did Jesus perform real miracles or did those events just appear to be miraculous at the time. Therefore, for this reason, and the reasons cited above, the Gospel accounts can be equally employed in establishing the historicity of Jesus.

Other New Testament Writers

The third reason in support of the historicity of Jesus is found in the writings of other New Testament authors. Among those additional sources who wrote about the historical Jesus of most interest for our study is Paul, more specifically his account of an early creedal statement found in 1 Corinthians chapter 15. Prior to that investigation, it is worth noting the view of many scholars, conservative and not, who hold to the perspective of additional sources that antedate the known New Testament literature. Simply asked, from where did the Gospel and Epistle writers gain their information? Licona points out, "Luke is clear that these sources existed when he wrote his Gospel and that he himself was dependent on other sources (Luke 1:1-3)."[38]

The Source "Q"

Form criticism has yielded what some scholars believe to be a source entitled Q. But Licona offers a cautious approach, "It is important to keep in mind that the existence of Q cannot be proven, since it is possible that Matthew and Luke received their information from a common witness (person) or oral traditions that had been carefully constructed about or even by Jesus and was then preserved."[39] The title Q serves as a placeholder for a document believed to be a collection of pre-Gospel literature from where the Evangelists gained a portion of their writings. This deduction is ascertained from a study of similarly phrased passages and stories that seem to match an identical independent source. Additional fields to plow in this area are the Pre-Markan tradition, the speeches in Acts, and other oral formulas throughout the New Testament writings.

Jesus, a Figure of Devotion

Larry Hurtado points out from a scholarly level, "The most remarkable innovation in first-century Christian circles [writing] was the inclusion of the risen/exalted Jesus as recipient of cultic devotion."[40] Hurtado continues on his thought mentioning that for historical purposes, "this is perhaps the most puzzling and

---

[38] Michael R. Licona, *The Resurrection of Jesus* (Downers Grove, IL: InterVarsity Press, 2010), 210.
[39] Ibid, 212.
[40] Larry W. Hurtado, *Jesus' Resurrection in the Early Christian Texts* (Thousand Oaks, CA: Journal of the Study of the Historical Jesus, 2005) Vol. 3.2, 205.

most notable feature of earliest Christian treatment of the figure of Jesus."[41] However, for the sake of space, I will move back to Paul's creedal statement (1 Corinthians 15:3-8).

The Creed

Paul is essential for two compelling reasons. He "claims to have known other leading disciples to whom the risen Jesus had appeared" and "He [Paul] is our earliest written source that mentions the resurrection of Jesus."[42] Scholars agree Paul's writings occurred sometime "between A.D. 48-65."[43] Some skeptical academics hold to a view that the Gospel writers fictionally inserted the empty tomb and a physically resurrected Jesus into their narratives. Since the Gospel narratives were written some thirty to sixty years after the death of Jesus, what evidence is there of an early account of a risen Jesus in bodily form?

The Evidence

Paul writes in the Corinthian text that *"I also received"* what he is about to write, that being an explicit reference to the death, burial, and resurrection of Jesus. We know Paul wrote his letter to the Corinthians in A.D. 55.[44] We additionally know, he visited the city of Corinth four years earlier in 51 A.D.[45] Paul affirms in the text that he *"received"* this creedal statement at an

---

[41] Ibid, 205.
[42] Michael R. Licona, *The Resurrection of Jesus* (Downers Grove, IL: InterVarsity Press, 2010), 208.
[43] Ibid, 208.
[44] Ibid, 223.
[45] Ibid, 223.

even earlier date. We know this by the statement "*I delivered to you as of first important what I also received.*" The question becomes, when and where did Paul receive this creedal statement? Most scholars attribute that date and location to be in Jerusalem sometime around A.D. 35-36,[46] based upon his Acts 9 conversion experience immediately following his three years in Damascus. Regarding Paul's visit to Jerusalem, Licona writes, "He [then] visited Jerusalem for the first time since his conversion experience (Gal. 1:18)."[47] While in Jerusalem, Paul visited with Peter and James to discuss their early eyewitness accounts of the resurrection. This early creedal statement from Paul and its connection to his first visit to Jerusalem are even recognized by atheist New Testament critic Gerd Ludemann as, "one of the great achievements of recent New Testament scholarship."[48] Licona concludes,

> *Virtually all critical scholars who have written on the subject, including rather skeptical ones, maintain that in 1 Corinthians 15:3-7 Paul has provided tradition(s) about Jesus that he did not form but rather received from others, as he claims. There is likewise widespread agreement that it was composed very early and may very well be the oldest extant tradition pertaining to the resurrection of Jesus.*[49]

It is important to note from a historical perspective that Paul was clearly antagonistic to the emerging Christian faith. Those who wish to discredit the authenticity of his writings must

---

[46] Ibid, 234.
[47] Ibid, 230.
[48] Ibid, 233.
[49] Ibid, 234.

first explain why a former antagonist would abandon the faith of his ancestors for a new fledgling and apparently heretical subsection of the Jewish faith. There simply is no evidence that Paul as a first rate philosopher and intellectual leader of his day would have any motivation to concoct false stories and lead his fellow Jews into a false teaching. Therefore, one can easily conclude from the authenticity of Paul and other New Testament writers that the historicity of Jesus is well founded.

A Culmination of Evidence

In closing, for one to place their confidence in the truth claims of Christianity, it must be established on rational grounds that the case for the historicity of Jesus is complete. With a sound foundational claim in trusting historical records, one is then free to entertain and explore the more profound and deeper elements of Jesus' claims, and not only His claims, but also His life, death, and proposed resurrection. Once the historicity of Jesus debate is settled, the heavy lifting of examining the best hypothesis for the empty tomb, appearances of Jesus to His disciples, and the origin of Christianity can ensue. On the path to the journey of finding the best explanation for the resurrection, we find three reasons that provide concrete footing while providing ample lighting on the road toward fully embracing the resurrection event.

- First, we reasoned extra-biblical sources provide extremely valid reasons to believe Jesus existed and not only existed but did so in a manner consistent with the biblical accounts. We discovered there is simply no good reason to conclude that first and second-century historians would have merely made up the Jesus account to support some mythical story parading around first-century Palestine.

- Second, we established additional backing for the historicity of Jesus by looking at the Gospel accounts as historical documents instead of divinely inspired writings. We found no good reason to conclude the independent writings on the accounts of Jesus' life are anything but reliable historical accounts based on real events that match other historical documents. The idea of separating out the inspiration discussion does not invalidate the belief in and of divine inspiration but rather aids one in a purely historical context. Once the historicity of Jesus and His resurrection is firmly established, it is within logical reason to attribute divine inspiration to Scripture and all that it entails.

- Third, we found good evidence from other, non-Gospel, New Testament writers who support the historicity of Jesus. The writings of Paul lend credibility to the historical veracity of these accounts, and again there is simply no good reason to dismiss the personal testimony of one who is willing to write and suffer for his belief in the accuracy of what has been written, especially if his former belief was antagonistic from the start.

In sum, with the historicity of Jesus firmly in place, one is free to roam through the field of resurrection hypotheses in search for the best explanation of the data of the empty tomb, post-mortem appearances of Jesus, and the origin of Christianity.

CHAPTER TWO
Data Crunching the Resurrection

A Most Significant Event

Imagine a singular event in which the magnitude of said event alters history in such a way as to leave an undeniable effect of its existence. In other words, the fact cannot be ignored. In modern historical terms, especially for those in the United States, one can easily recall the events of September 11, 2001. Even today, the effect of this one single event is persistently shifting and changing our world. As we look further back into history, one can undoubtedly conclude July 4, 1776, as the day Western democracy was born. Similarly, Christianity can trace its origin to a singular event dated during the Jewish Passover of A.D. 30 or 33 in the city of Jerusalem.[50] Without a doubt, from the genesis of the resurrection event of Jesus of Nazareth, fictitious or not, our world was forever changed. Of interest to this essay is the nature of the fictitiousness of the event. In other words, is Richard Carrier correct in assessing, "As a professional historian, I do not believe we have anywhere near sufficient evidence or reason to believe this [the resurrection of Jesus]?"[51]

The effect [of the resurrection] is without a doubt; however, of most significance is whether or not the event, meaning historically, took place. For if true, it follows Jesus is who He said He was and belief in Him begins the road to eternal life.[52] Even though skeptics may argue the resurrection of Jesus is nothing more than fiction, I will argue there are real data to provide reasonable belief in the resurrection event as historically told by those who witnessed it, thereby providing confidence in the truthfulness of the claim and more importantly assurance to those who believe in eternal life.

Crunching Data

In truth, one can approach the accuracy of the resurrection event from an experiential or historical approach. Unfortunately,

---

[50] We say A.D. 30 or 33 due to a general scholarly consensus between these two dates. Andreas Köstenberger holds to the A.D. 33 date yet summarizes, "We conclude that Jesus was most likely crucified on April 3, A.D. 33. While other dates are possible, believers can take great assurance from the fact that the most important historical events in Jesus's life, such as the crucifixion, are firmly anchored in human history." Accessed, May 1, 2017; https://www.firstthings.com/web-exclusives/2014/04/april-3-ad-33.

[51] https://infidels.org/library/modern/richard_carrier/resurrection/lecture.html. Accessed May 3, 2017.

[52] N.T. Wright, *The Resurrection of the Son of God* (Minneapolis, MN: Fortress Press, 2003), 355.

the experiential approach is burdened with a lack of hard data to uphold the declaration, thereby leaving the fictitiousness of the event in question. Fortunately, the historical approach uses data to remove proposed fictional elements in an attempt to leave us with facts, thereby the truth.

Interestingly, modern historians have begun to call on the emerging field of Big Data to aggregate information with hopes of finding the past and predicting the future. In February of 2012, the New York Times declared, "We have entered the Age of Big Data."[53] In referencing information data points as "signals," James Grossman, Executive Director of the American Historical Association writes, "Decoding these signals [data points] is historical work: untangling their true meanings requires proper analysis of their context. To study these signals is to study change—to figure out how change happens—which is what historians do best."[54] It is an intriguing possibility to utilize historical data points in a similar fashion as a modern-day data crunch in finding truth or patterns to events past and present.

In respect to Christianity, what event occurred that caused such a rapid change within established second-Temple Judaism? Historically, we understand early followers of Jesus claimed it was His bodily resurrection from the dead that served as the catalyst for their belief. However, we need to establish the historical data

---

[53] http://www.nytimes.com/2012/02/12/sunday-review/big-datas-impact-in-the-world.html. Accessed May 2, 2017
[54] https://www.historians.org/publications-and-directories/perspectives-on-history/march-2012/big-data-an-opportunity-for-historians. Accessed May 3, 2017.

points for what drove this view in hopes of better understanding their mindset and the potential for its reality.

Points of Agreement

For this inquiry, I will utilize three generally accepted data points from the first century and '*crunch the information*' in hopes of uncovering the truth to Christianity's resurrection claim. About the three accepted data points, Michael Licona writes, "Some facts are so strongly evidenced that they are virtually indisputable."[55] Those three data points are:

- The Empty Tomb
- The Resurrection Appearances
- The Origin of the Christian Faith

Of interest to the resurrection debate, Gary Habermas has developed a minimal fact approach in which he has collected a treasure trove of over 3,400 academic sources from skeptical to conservative scholarship, "written on the subject of Jesus resurrection from 1975 to the present in German, French and English."[56] While this is an impressive set of data, it does not necessarily prove the resurrection event to be true, but rather according to Habermas, does give us "some clues as to where recent scholars think the data point."[57]

---

[55] Michael R. Licona, *The Resurrection of Jesus* (Nottingham, England: IVP Academic, 2010), 56.
[56] Ibid, 278.
[57] Habermas in Norman L. Geisler and Chad V. Meister, *Reasons for Faith: Making a Case for the Christian Faith* (Wheaton, IL: Crossway Books, 2007), 282.

It is important to note that according to Habermas, Licona, and Craig, conservative, liberal, and skeptical scholars alike generally accept these three data points as "historical bedrock."[58] William Lane Craig concludes by commenting, "If these three facts can be established and no plausible natural explanation can account for them as well as the resurrection hypothesis, then one is justified in inferring Jesus' resurrection as the most plausible explanation of the data."[59]

Lastly, prior to a more detailed analysis of the data, it is important to note that each person approaches the evidence and data from a particular point of view. As Craig says, "One doesn't come to a historical investigation of Jesus' resurrection in a vacuum."[60]

My Approach

In agreement with Craig, I approach this exploration with the premise that God exists as exhibited by the weight of natural theology. Classical arguments such at the cosmological, moral, teleological, and ontological argument provide reasonable proof for the presupposition that God exists. Because the atheist, pantheist, Hindu, Buddhist, or agnostic presupposes the opposite belief in God's existence, I will leave it up to them to provide convincing proof of the non-existence of God prior to offering a

---

[58] Michael R. Licona, *The Resurrection of Jesus* (Nottingham, England: IVP Academic, 2010), 278.
[59] W.L. Craig, seminar entitled, *The Historical Jesus & The Resurrection* (Atlanta, Georgia), April 7-8, 2017.
[60] Craig, *The Historical Jesus & The Resurrection* (Atlanta, Georgia), April 7-8, 2017.

competing conclusion to our investigation. Having said that, let us evaluate the substantiation of these three data.

Data Point One: The Empty Tomb

One of the most certain data points in support of the resurrection claim is the empty tomb. According to the earliest Gospel accounts on the first Sunday following the Friday crucifixion of Jesus, a group of women followers found the tomb of Jesus empty, meaning Jesus' body was not there. From this core belief of an empty tomb, the resurrection pronouncement was codified. N.T. Wright points out that, "the world of second-Temple Judaism supplied the concept of resurrection, but the striking and consistent Christian mutations within Jewish resurrection belief rule out any possibility that the belief could have generated spontaneously from within its Jewish context."[61] Simply put, something must have driven the belief in an empty tomb. There are three facts to support the tomb of Jesus was empty as the Gospel accounts indicate.[62]

The Burial

First, the historical reliability of Jesus' burial supports the empty tomb. Why? Because knowing the location of the burial of Jesus would have easily disproved the empty tomb claim if indeed Jesus' body was still there. This means the tomb of Jesus would

---

[61] N.T. Wright, *The Resurrection of the Son of God* (Minneapolis, MN: Fortress Press, 2003), 355.
[62] W.L. Craig, seminar entitled, *The Historical Jesus & The Resurrection* (Atlanta, Georgia), April 7-8, 2017.

have to be empty if the disciples wanted their story to have any impact. Even if the disciples preached about a risen Jesus, they would be hard pressed to gain any followers if the tomb was still occupied. Craig comments, "One of the most remarkable facts about the early Christian belief in Jesus' resurrection was that it flourished in the very city where Jesus had been publicly crucified. So long as the people of Jerusalem thought that Jesus' body was in the tomb, few would have been prepared to believe such nonsense as that Jesus had been raised from the dead."[63]

Additionally, even if the disciples could have won some converts, the Jewish authorities had great motivation to stamp out this upstart religious movement. In fact, the employment of Saul of Tarsus to persecute initial Christian development supports this notion. In truth, however, we have no such evidence of Jewish or other authorities providing any claim of Jesus' body still in the tomb. Thus, what confidence do we have that Jesus was actually buried and knowledge of His tomb was available at the time? Remarkably, according to agnostic-leaning atheist, Bart Ehrman, "the earliest accounts we have are unanimous in saying that Jesus was in fact buried by this fellow, Joseph of Arimathea, and so it's relatively reliable that that's what happened. We also have solid traditions to indicate that women found this tomb empty three days later.[64] Craig Evans likewise points out that understanding the Jewish burial traditions of antiquity almost inescapably confirms Jesus was in fact appropriately buried immediately following the

---

[63] Craig, seminar, *The Historical Jesus & The Resurrection*
[64] Bart Ehrman, "From Jesus to Constantine: A History of Early Christianity," Lecture 4: "Oral and Written Traditions about Jesus" (The Teaching Company, 2003).

crucifixion event. Evans writes, "Quite apart from any concerns with the deceased men or their families, the major concern would have had to do with the defilement of the land and the holy city."[65] Evans concludes his scholarly piece by commenting,

> *It is very probable that Jesus was buried, in keeping with Jewish customs... some of Jesus' followers (such as the women mentioned in the Gospel accounts) knew where Jesus' body had been placed and intended to mark the location, perfume his body, and mourn, in keeping with Jewish customs. The intention was to take possession of Jesus' remains, at some point in the future, and transfer them to his family burial place.*[66]

Lastly, we have multiple independent testimonies referring to Joseph of Arimathea and the burial of Jesus in the apostolic sermons located in the book of Acts, the writings of Paul, the Gospel accounts of Mark, John, and the sources behind Matthew and Luke. For those who wish to deny the burial account of Jesus, sadly for their assessment, they are decisively against the mainstream of scholarly understanding in this area. According to the late John A. T. Robinson of Cambridge University, the burial of Jesus in the tomb is "one of the earliest and best-attested facts about Jesus."[67] Because of the above-mentioned convincing authentication, it is hard to deny the historical data of Jesus' burial supporting the empty tomb.

---

[65] Craig A. Evans, *Jewish Burial Traditions and the Resurrection of Jesus* (Thousand Oaks, CA: Journal for the Study of the Historical Jesus Vol. 3.2, SAGE Publications, 2005), 241.
[66] Ibid, 247-248.
[67] John A. T. Robinson, *The Human Face of God* (Philadelphia, PA: Westminster, 1973), 131.

The Discovery

Second, the discovery of Jesus' empty tomb is attested in very early, independent sources. In similar fashion as the burial account, there is a common theme within the same source materials for the empty tomb. Even though there is a common theme, it is important to note the skeptic's argument that, "however numerous the independent source[s] may be, this establishes only the age of a tradition, not its authenticity."[68] Therefore, we are not arguing multiple attestations as the only proof in establishing reliability historically; however, we can support multiple attestations that give us additional data to crunch. We are only attempting to create here the historical tradition of the empty tomb as believed and taught by the early leaders of Christianity.

Simply put, the encounter of Jesus' empty tomb cannot be considered a late mythical legend. The pre-Markan Passion source, I Corinthians 15:3-5, Matthew's independent source, John, Luke, and Acts all affirm an early tradition of the empty tomb. Nevertheless, skeptics such as Dale Allison argue although Paul [and the others] may have believed in the empty tomb on theological grounds, he [they] may not have had actual historical knowledge of it.[69] Yet, Craig counters this skepticism by mentioning, "The idea that a man could be buried and then be raised from the dead and yet his body still remain in the grave is a peculiarly modern notion. For first century Jews there would have

---

[68] Theissen and Winter, *Quest for the Plausible Jesus* (Edinburgh, Scotland: T&T Clark, 1906; 3rd ed, 1911), 14-15.
[69] Dale C. Allison, *Resurrecting Jesus* (New York, NY: T&T Clark, 2005), 316.

been no question but that the tomb of Jesus would have been empty."[70]

Therefore, similar to a surplus of witnesses in a court of law, the corroborating nature of multiple independent acknowledgments is challenging to reject, and we are on reasonable footing to utilize multiple attestation testimonies as additional data to crunch.

Women as the First Witnesses

Third, women discovered the tomb empty. According to Gary Habermas, "By far the most popular argument favoring the Gospel testimony on this subject [the empty tomb] is that, in all four texts, women are listed as the initial witnesses."[71] This is of significant interest on account of historical accuracy within first-century Mediterranean culture regarding the general reluctance to accept female testimony in legal matters. In fact, Josephus gives an account regarding admissible testimony: "Let not the testimony of women be admitted, on account of the levity and boldness of their sex" (*Antiquities of the Jews* IV.8.15.§219). This statement is an echo of the "patriarchal society of first century Judaism."[72]

Simply put, if women were not true first witnesses of the empty tomb, it makes no sense for early Christian writers to

---

[70] W.L. Craig, seminar entitled, *The Historical Jesus & The Resurrection* (Atlanta, Georgia), April 7-8, 2017.
[71] Gary R. Habermas, *Resurrection Research from 1975 to the Present* (Thousand Oaks, CA: Journal for the Study of the Historical Jesus, Vol. 3.2, SAGE Publications, 2005), 141.
[72] W.L. Craig, seminar entitled, *The Historical Jesus & The Resurrection* (Atlanta, Georgia), April 7-8, 2017.

superimpose the least credible candidates as their star witnesses unless it was true. Skeptics have devised all sorts of dubious hypotheses as to why the Gospel writers list women as the first witnesses. However, there has yet to be a convincing reason to compete with only taking the early writers at their word. In fact, William Lane Craig comments, "No other factor has proved so persuasive to scholars of the empty tomb's historicity as the role of the female witnesses." Habermas concludes from his 3,400 academically based source material, "of those scholars who comment on the subject [most] hold that the Gospels probably would not have dubbed them as the chief witnesses unless they actually did attest to this event."[73] Therefore, we can resolve there is additional overwhelming data supported by the testimony of female witnesses regarding the empty tomb. In sum, as a collection of data points, the burial of Jesus, early and multiple independent attestations, and the testimony of women as first witnesses symphonically combine in support of an empty tomb.

Data Point Two:
The Resurrection Appearances

A secondary data point in support of the resurrection claim is found in the multiple eyewitness testimonies of the appearances of Jesus. In attempting to discover the historical truth of the resurrection event, one must not only consider the substantial evidence for the empty tomb, but one also needs to

---

[73] Ibid, 141.

factor in the claim that Jesus' earliest followers declared to have seen Him alive in bodily form after His execution. There are three lines of evidence in support of the post-mortem appearances of Jesus.

List of Appearances

First, Paul's list of appearances in 1 Corinthians 15 provides a certifiable database regarding the claim. Not only do Paul and other New Testament writers endorse this list, but moreover it can be tested by doubters. This testability feature provided to us by the early followers lends high psychological credibility to their belief in the appearances at the time. Furthermore, a scholarly literary examination of the Pauline manuscript strongly indicates it was authored by Paul in A.D. 54-55,[74] and this smaller portion of his larger text is an early creedal statement given to him sometime in the mid A.D. 30's from Peter and James.[75] So here we have a very early account, three to five years from the resurrection event, provided by eyewitnesses who claim to have seen Jesus alive on the first Sunday after his Friday crucifixion.

In 1 Corinthians 15:3-8, Paul writes:

> *For I delivered to you as of first importance what I also received,*
> > *that Christ died for our sins in*
> > > *accordance with the scriptures,*
> > *and that he was buried,*
> > *and that he was raised on the third day in*

---

[74] Michael R. Licona, *The Resurrection of Jesus* (Downers Grove, IL: InterVarsity Press, 2010), 208.
[75] Ibid, 234.

> *accordance with the scriptures, and that he appeared to Cephas, then to the Twelve.*
>
> *Then he appeared to more than five hundred brethren at one time, most of whom are still alive, though some have fallen asleep. Then he appeared to James, then to all the apostles. Last of all, as to one untimely born, he appeared also to me.*

Testable

As mentioned, this list is testable. Let us test the appearance to Peter. First, both this account and the account in Luke 24:34 are cited in an older Christian tradition. We know this by the use of the name "Cephas" by Paul and the name "Simon" by Luke. Second, William Lane Craig points out, "That Luke is working with a tradition here is evident by the awkward way in which it intrudes into his narrative of the Emmaus disciples... it is quite well founded historically. As a result, even the most skeptical New Testament critics agree that Peter saw an appearance of Jesus alive from the dead."[76] Lastly, Paul testifies in Galatians 1:18 that he spent about two weeks in Jerusalem three years after his Damascus Road encounter with the risen Jesus. Paul is in the unique position to know for certain if Peter claimed to have an experience with the resurrected Jesus or not. Of most interest is the fact that those specifically named on Paul's list could have been interviewed or *"fact checked"* by any interested party at the time. In truth, we have no contrary documents stating opposing views to Paul's list. Historically, this is very secure data

---

[76] W.L. Craig, seminar entitled, *The Historical Jesus & The Resurrection* (Atlanta, Georgia), April 7-8, 2017.

to include in a fair-minded exploration of the facts. We do not have room to investigate and offer supporting data for the other Pauline-certified appearances, however similar qualified information is available for each instance listed above.

Multiple Independent Accounts

The second line of evidence in support of the post-mortem appearances of Jesus is the multiple, independent attestations from the Gospel accounts. Not only does Paul mention the Twelve in his early creedal statement but Luke and John corroborate Jesus' appearance to the same group as well (Luke 24:36-43; John 20:19-20). Moreover, Matthew and John separately declare the women followers as seeing Jesus alive after His crucifixion (Matthew 28:9-10; John 20:11-17). Craig believes due to the criterion of embarrassment, we can be even more confident in the actuality of Matthew and John's claim. He writes, "It is generally agreed that the absence of this appearance from the list of appearances in the tradition quoted by Paul is a reflection of the same discomfort in citing female witnesses;" [77] therefore, this discomfort lends credibility to its historicity.

Lastly, Mark, Matthew, and John all independently confirm that Jesus appeared to His disciples in Galilee (Mark 16:7; Matthew 28:16-17; Jn. 21). Of note, Craig points out, "Taken sequentially, the appearances follow the pattern of Jerusalem—Galilee—Jerusalem, matching the festival pilgrimages of the disciples as they returned to Galilee following the Passover/Feast

---

[77] Ibid.

of Unleavened Bread and traveled again to Jerusalem two months later for Pentecost."[78] Bundled jointly, we now have added data points to crunch in our pursuit.

Critics Agree

Remarkably, the appearances are so well evidenced, even critics grant the idea that Jesus' earliest followers believed they saw Jesus as the risen Christ. In fact, New Testament critic Norman Perrin states, "The more we study the tradition with regard to the appearances, the firmer the rock begins to appear upon which they are based."[79] Not to be outdone, atheist historian Gerd Lüdemann pens, "It may be taken as historically certain that Peter and the disciples had experiences after Jesus' death in which Jesus appeared to them as the risen Christ."[80] The question is now raised, what type of appearances were these; visions, apparitions, hallucinations, physical bodily appearances, or something else? Let us go directly to the sources and find out what the early disciples claimed these appearances to be. After all, historically, this is their testimony, and they were the ones with an exclusive perspective to tell us what they experienced and saw.

The Nature of His Appearances

The third line of reasoning regarding the manifestations of Jesus is related to the nature of His appearances. There is debate between New Testament scholarship as to the type or kind of

---

[78] Ibid.
[79] Norman Perrin, *The Resurrection According to Matthew, Mark, and Luke* (Philadelphia, PA: Fortress, 1974), 80.
[80] Gerd Lüdemann, *What Really Happened to Jesus?* (Louisville, KY: Westminster John Knox Press, 1995), 80.

appearances the early followers claimed to see. However, both Paul and the Gospel writers clearly imply and describe the appearances of Jesus to be in bodily form. Paul unmistakably teaches in 1 Corinthians 15:42-44 that believers can be confident not only in the immortality of the soul but also in the resurrection of their physical body.[81] Paul taught this uniquely new Christian doctrine on account of his personal encounter with the risen Jesus (Acts 9). Regarding Paul's perspective and teaching on Jesus' resurrection, N.T. Wright concludes Paul firmly believed, "His [Jesus] body had not been abandoned in the tomb. Nor had it merely been resuscitated, coming back into a more or less identical life, to face death again at some point in the future. It had been transformed, changed, in an act of new creation through which it was no longer corruptible."[82] Michael Licona, in his 650-page tome, after providing page after page of incredibly deep and robust scholarly work on this subject and Paul's belief in our future bodily resurrection, confidently proclaims, "We have looked carefully at a number of Pauline passage and have observed that Paul never regarded the final postmortem state of believers to be one of disembodiment."[83]

Visions or Appearances

It is additionally important to note that there is a clear New Testament distinction between appearances of Jesus in bodily

---

[81] W.L. Craig, seminar entitled, *The Historical Jesus & The Resurrection* (Atlanta, Georgia), April 7-8, 2017.
[82] N.T. Wright, *The Resurrection of the Son of God* (Minneapolis, MN: Fortress Press, 2003), 361.
[83] Michael R. Licona, *The Resurrection of Jesus* (Downers Grove, IL: InterVarsity Press, 2010), 436.

form and visions of Jesus existing in the mind of an individual believer. For example, Stephen's vision of Jesus in Acts 7 is described in an entirely different fashion as Paul's Damascus Road appearance in Acts 9. Additionally, the Gospel appearances of Jesus' physical interaction with His followers is described completely different from Paul's third heaven experience found in 2 Corinthians 12. Luke describes Stephen as the only person who could see and interact with Jesus in his vision while he describes Paul and his travel companions as all experiencing, albeit at different levels, the effect of an appearance that was "out there."[84]

The same is true in the Gospel accounts regarding the disciples touching Jesus, eating breakfast with Him, and interacting with His teaching. These are clear examples of real world experiences that the Gospel writers describe as true to life events not apparitions, hallucination, or imaginary events. Craig summarizes,

> *To be perfectly candid, the only grounds for denying the physical, corporeal nature of the post-mortem appearances of Jesus is philosophical, not historical: such appearances would be nature miracles of the most stupendous proportions, and that many critics cannot swallow. But in that case, one needs to re-trace one's steps to think again about the existence of God and the problem of miracles. Most New Testament critics are untrained in philosophy and are, hence, naive when it comes to these issues.*[85]

---

[84] W.L. Craig, seminar entitled, *The Historical Jesus & The Resurrection* (Atlanta, Georgia), April 7-8, 2017.
[85] W.L. Craig, *Reasonable Faith: Christian Truth and Apologetics,* Third Ed. (Wheaton, IL: Crossway, 2008), 384.

In sum, regarding this second data point, we have multiple individuals experiencing post-mortem appearances of Jesus in a physical bodily form different from visions, hallucinations, or other types. These experiences are numerous and are independently attested to in a historically reliable way. Therefore, we are within reason to include as additional data points, these three lines of reasoning mentioned above in support of the post-mortem appearances of Jesus.

Data Point Three: The Origin of the Christian Faith

The third data point in support of the resurrection claim is found in the rapid formation of Christianity as a departure from historical Judaism. Larry Hurtado points out from a scholarly level, "The most remarkable innovation in first-century Christian circles was the inclusion of the risen/exalted Jesus as recipient of cultic devotion."[86] Hurtado continues on his thought mentioning that for historical purposes, "this is perhaps the most puzzling and most notable feature of earliest Christian treatment of the figure of Jesus."[87] Simply put, Jewish devotees of any particular cultural influencer never viewed individual spiritual or military leaders as Divinity. To do so would be blasphemous. Yet, in the case of Jesus, this is exactly what happened, and we have no similar Jewish historical example to compare His exaltation to. History

---

[86] Larry W. Hurtado, *Jesus' Resurrection in the Early Christian Texts* (Thousand Oaks, CA: Journal of the Study of the Historical Jesus, 2005) Vol. 3.2, 205.
[87] Ibid, 205.

begs the question as to why did His early Jewish followers, shortly after the crucifixion, proclaim Him as Lord? This is completely un-Jewish in the strongest sense of the word.

Jesus Declared as God

In fact, we see incredible Jewish outrage in the stoning of Stephen and in the persecution of other early Christian leaders who preached Jesus as Lord. Fortunately, because of the literature of the New Testament, we know what the driving force behind the origin of the Christian faith was. For instance, in Acts 2:23, 36, regarding the fundamental change that took place in the lives of the followers of Jesus, Peter proclaims, "This Man . . . God raised . . . again . . . let all the house of Israel know for certain that God has made Him both Lord and Christ—this Jesus whom you crucified." According to the literature [data], this surprising turn of events from Peter's denial of knowing Jesus a few weeks earlier was driven by his encounter with a risen Jesus.

The Crucifixion Should Have Been Devastating

By far, the best treatment on this particular subject of the fundamental shift in Jewish thinking to early Christian thinking is offered in N.T. Wright's masterful work entitled *The Resurrection of the Son of God*. In this volume, Wright reveals the context in which Jesus was viewed by the people of His day. For them, "The crucifixion of Jesus, understood from the point of view of any onlooker, whether sympathetic or not, was bound to have appeared as the complete destruction of any messianic pretensions or possibilities he or his followers might have hinted at."[88] The idea of a Messiah who was defeated by Rome at the hands of Jewish leaders was entirely foreign to those early disciples. When Jesus was crucified, simply put, all hope was gone. Craig comments, "Messiah was supposed to be a triumphant figure who would command the respect of Jew and Gentile alike and who would establish the throne of David in Jerusalem. A Messiah who failed to deliver and to reign, who was defeated, humiliated, and slain by his enemies, is a contradiction in terms."[89] However, from a sheer historical point of view, it cannot be denied that belief in the resurrection of Jesus "reversed the catastrophe of the crucifixion."[90] The universal belief and teaching within the foundational years of the early Christian community undoubtedly were driven by their unwavering belief in Jesus as the risen Lord.

Finally, not to be overlooked, the commonality of the resurrection narrative among Jewish and Gentile communities is not easily missed, "What Paul preached was never the subject of controversy between Paul's Gentile mission and the church in Jerusalem. Jesus' death and resurrection was the event upon which their common proclamation was based."[91] In sum, regarding this third data point, we have the origin of the Christian faith driven by the resurrection of Jesus in stark contrast to generations of explicit Jewish teaching to the contrary. The exhaltation of Jesus as Lord is a major data point that should not be miscalculated.

---

[88] N.T. Wright, *The Resurrection of the Son of God* (Minneapolis, MN: Fortress Press, 2003), 557-8.
[89] W.L. Craig, seminar entitled, *The Historical Jesus & The Resurrection* (Atlanta, Georgia), April 7-8, 2017.
[90] Ibid.
[91] Helmut Koester, *Ancient Christian Gospels: Their History and Development* (London, Eng.: SCM, 1990), 51.

The Final Crunch

We now need to compile all the data regarding the resurrection claim in search for the best explanation for the empty tomb, resurrection appearances of Jesus, and the origin of Christianity.

- We can determine the burial of Jesus, early and multiple independent attestations, and the testimony of women as first witnesses symphonically combine in support of an empty tomb.

- Secondly, we have various individuals experiencing post-mortem appearances of Jesus in a physical bodily form different from visions, hallucinations, or other types. These experiences are numerous and are independently attested to in a historically reliable way.
- Finally, we have the origin of the Christian faith driven by the resurrection of Jesus in stark contrast to generations of explicit Jewish teaching with the exaltation of Jesus as Lord providing the driving force to the origin of the Christian faith.

As R. H. Fuller says, even the most skeptical critic must posit some mysterious "X" to get the movement going.[92] As we crunch the data, it seems to me one is within excellent grounds from a historical and experiential perspective to conclude that it is

---

[92] R. H. Fuller, *The Formation of the Resurrection Narratives* (London, Eng.: SPCK, 1972), 2.

very likely that in fact Jesus rose from the dead in bodily form and the events as told by the early followers of Jesus are true. Unless and until a better "X" is provided for the data, I hold firm to the conclusion that Jesus is Lord and the early followers got it right as recorded in the literature of the New Testament.

T.K. Anderson

CHAPTER THREE
The Hallucination Theory

Did The Disciples Hallucinate the Resurrection?

Circa 55 A.D. Paul wrote to the Christians in the city of Corinth,[93] "...if Christ has not been raised, our preaching is useless and so is your faith. More than that, we are then found to be false witnesses about God, for we have testified about God that he raised Christ from the dead."[94] Thus, from its roots, Jesus' followers proclaimed that He indeed rose from the dead.[95] Christianity and the story of the bodily resurrection of Jesus spread

---

[93] Clinton E. Arnold and David W.J. Gill, *Zondervan Illustrated Bible Backgrounds Commentary Volume 3* (Grand Rapids, MI; Zondervan, 2002), 108.
[94] Holy Bible, New International Version, NIV Copyright 1973, 1978, 1984, 2011, accessed September 24, 2014,
https://www.biblegateway.com/passage/?search=1+Corinthians+15&version=NIV.
[95] William L. Craig, *Doctrine of Christ (part 17)*, accessed October 4, 2014, http://www.reasonablefaith.org/defenders-2-podcast/transcript/s6-17.

rapidly throughout the Roman world. What could account for this rapid rise of Christianity? Did Jesus' earliest followers really see Him alive after His crucifixion? Well, today, most skeptics argue that the disciples' proclamation in the bodily resurrection of Jesus was only the result of their hallucinating the resurrection appearances.[96] But they are mistaken. It seems to me, the hallucination theory is not able to bear the weight of historical evidence or current understanding of hallucinatory events.

Understanding The Mind

First, modern psychology supports the idea that hallucinations are individual and subjective not group oriented. Clinical Psychologist Dr. Gary Collins says,

> *Hallucinations are individual occurrences. By their very nature only one person can see a given hallucination at a time. They certainly aren't something, which can be seen by a group of people. Neither is it possible that one person could somehow induce a hallucination in somebody else. Since a hallucination exists only in this subjective, personal sense, it is obvious that others cannot witness it.*[97]

In support of Collins' position, Dr. Gary Habermas concludes almost all psychologists dispute the possibility of the central claim of this theory, that a group of people can witness the same

---

[96] Gary Habermas, *Explaining Away Jesus' Resurrection: Hallucination*, accessed September 23, 2014, http://www.equip.org/articles/explaining-away-jesus-resurrection-hallucination/#christian-books-1.

[97] Gary Collins, quoted in Lee Strobel, *The Case for Christ* (Grand Rapids, MI; Zondervan Publishing House, 1998), 322.

hallucination.⁹⁸ Additionally, hallucinations are short in time. These suggested hallucinations happened over a period of 40 days and stopped suddenly. Furthermore, Jesus' appearances to multiple people, in multiple locations, over a long period of time contradict the normal structure of hallucination events. Likewise, Jesus' disciples were fearful and disbelieving. Hallucinations take place in a field of expectancy. These disciples were not expecting Jesus to come back from the dead.⁹⁹ Finally, one is not able to reach out and touch, or eat with, a hallucination as the early followers claimed they did with Jesus.

Groupthink

What about the idea of groupthink? Is it possible that Jesus' early followers fooled themselves into believing? Skeptic Michael Martin wrote, "A person full of religious zeal may see what he or she wants to see, not what is really there."¹⁰⁰ Perhaps the disciples projected what they wanted to be true instead of what was actually true. Remarkably, even atheist turned deist, Antony Flew, doesn't buy into this ideology. In a debate with Dr. Habermas, Dr. Flew commented, "I don't like it when other atheists use that argument, because it cuts both ways. Christians believe because they want to, but atheists don't believe because they don't want to!"¹⁰¹ Groupthink does not account for the empty tomb, the conversions of Paul and James the brother of Jesus, or

---

[98] Gary Habermas, *Explaining Away Jesus' Resurrection: Hallucination*, accessed September 22, 2014, http://www.equip.org/articles/explaining-away-jesus-resurrection-hallucination/#christian-books-1.
[99] Lee Strobel, *The Case for Christ* (Grand Rapids, MI; Zondervan Publishing House, 1998), 323.
[100] Ibid. 323. Martin, *The Case against Christianity*, 75.
[101] Ibid. 323.

the foundational faith of these early followers that were willing to die for their belief in a resurrected Jesus.

Delusions

How about a delusion theory? If it was not groupthink, maybe the early leaders of Christianity tricked the early followers? Perhaps it was something similar to the Marshall Applewhite phenomenon of the Church of Venus a few years ago. Author Lee Strobel presented this theory to Dr. Mike Licona, "We could postulate the theory that Peter saw a hallucination of Jesus and then he convinced the other disciples—he deluded them—into believing Jesus had risen from the dead."[102] Licona simply responded with "it doesn't account for all the facts."[103]

Again, much like the idea of groupthink, the idea of Peter creating a delusion would not account for somebody checking out the tomb to see if Jesus' body was still there or the conversions of known skeptics. It could account for some of the early, small and internal group of followers, but it does not account for all of the facts; therefore, according to Dr. Licona, "It's not a good historical theory."[104]

The Empty Tomb

---

[102] Lee Strobel, *The Case for the Real Jesus* (Grand Rapids, MI; Zondervan Publishing House, 1998), 143.
[103] Ibid. 143.
[104] Ibid. 144.

A second problem for the hallucination theory is Jesus' empty tomb. First century skeptics could have easily investigated the tomb of Jesus and quickly suppressed the fledgling faith of these early Christians. It would have been difficult for the early followers of Jesus to spread a message of bodily resurrection if the tomb of Jesus was still occupied with His corpse. The fact that Jesus' tomb was empty and those living at the time could verify it, gave tremendous confidence to those early followers to boldly proclaim their Messiah had indeed risen from the grave.

The Passover Plot

Not so fast, says the modern day skeptic; what if Dr. Hugh Schonfield's 1965 book *The Passover Plot* is correct? In this book, he claims to offer a solution to the empty tomb. He speculates that Joseph of Arimathea was guided by Jesus to remove His body from the tomb so that the disciples would be convinced that He indeed rose from the dead. And by doing so, it would allow Jesus to be seen as the Messiah. The resurrection appearances are simple cases of mistaken identity.[105] However, this theory gives no reasons for the actual appearances of Jesus. Certainly, Peter, James, Mary, John, and others would have noticed the difference between Jesus and a stranger. Furthermore, Joseph of Arimathea was a devout Jew[106] and would not have broken the Sabbath by moving Jesus' body on Saturday. The opportunity and motives are in question with this notion. The Roman guards were present, Friday to Sunday, to guard the tomb

---

[105] Norman L. Geisler, *When Skeptics Ask* (Grand Rapids, MI; Baker Books, 1990), 124.
[106] Norman L. Geisler, *When Skeptics Ask* (Grand Rapids, MI; Baker Books, 1990), 123.

and the women came very early in the morning on Sunday. And the testimony of the grave clothes being left behind make this theory unacceptable. Lastly, where would he have stored the body? Would not someone have seen it and testified that Joseph took it?

Stolen Body

Nevertheless, what if someone else stole the body of Jesus from the tomb? What if the disciples stole the body, or what if the authorities stole the body of Jesus? Skeptics argue that this is a plausible explanation for the empty tomb. In the dark of the night, the disciples overpowered the Roman guards and rolled back the tombstone. They carted or carried Jesus' dead body to another burial place. Now, with the tomb being empty, they could proclaim that He rose from the dead.

Not possible. The disciples didn't have the power, and the authorities didn't have the motive.[107] The Roman guards of the tomb would not have been overpowered by a confused, disheveled, and disorganized group of Jesus' followers. With Jesus' death taking place Friday afternoon and most disciples fleeing in distress, the remaining followers lacked the courage to step close to Jesus' burial location for fear of their own execution. In fact, the gospel accounts emphasize this fact. Female followers arrived at Jesus' tomb on Easter morning, not the male disciples. If they were too afraid or discouraged to go in the early morning

---

[107] Josh McDowell, *The New Evidence that Demands a Verdict* (Nashville, TN; Thomas Nelson, 1999), 264.

hours to finish the burial sequence, it's highly doubtful they would have created a stealth attack on the Roman guards to steal Jesus' body. On the other hand, if the authorities stole the body, they would have simply produced it when these early disciples started to publically share that Jesus was risen from the dead. Furthermore, the authorities had no motive for stealing the body of Jesus.

Conversion of Skeptics

Thirdly, one of the most difficult answers to supply for modern-day hallucination theorists is the conversion of Saul of Tarsus and James, the younger brother of Jesus. This is a real problem for those who hold to the hallucination theory. There is no evidence that James, who was skeptical of Jesus' divinity, and Paul, who was a former persecutor of Christians, wanted anything to do with Jesus and His message. The retort from Jack Kent in an article written by Habermas states,

> *Paul was suffering from a Conversion Disorder, a psychological condition characterized by such physical symptoms as blindness or paralysis in the absence of specific neurological or medical causes. This was brought about by his inner turbulence, conflict, doubt, and guilt. Michael Goulder agrees about Paul, but adds that Peter and others, including perhaps James, were also suffering from the same problem.*[108]

---

[108] Gary Habermas, *Explaining Away Jesus' Resurrection: Hallucination*, accessed September 25, 2014, http://www.equip.org/articles/explaining-away-jesus-resurrection-hallucination/#christian-books-1.

There are a few problems with this analysis. Paul was the only individual to have shown these types of symptoms. When Goulder involves Peter, James, and possibly the others, he is simply not based in facts. Conversion disorders are most often found in women (up to 500% more likely), teenagers and young adults, military or combat individuals, people with lower I.Q.s or low socioeconomic status, and less-educated persons. [109] Interestingly, not a single trait applies to Paul and it would be extremely problematic to evidence them for Peter and James. In fact, Habermas writes,

> *Charging that these apostles were victims of conversion disorder simply does not fit the facts. It is clearly an over-reliance on a hypothesis apart from the data, a theory not anchored to reality. It would be highly improbable for all the necessary factors to converge simultaneously. Like the charge of mass hallucinations, it spawns more difficulties that it tries to solve.*[110]

A Radically New Concept

The fourth problem for the hallucination hypothesis centers on the state of mind for first-century Jewish believers. First-century Jewish believers would not have created the concept of a bodily, flesh and bone, earthly resurrection event. It was not a part of their thinking or belief concerning the afterlife. To say the early followers of Jesus arbitrarily hallucinated the appearances

---

[109] Ibid.
[110] Ibid.

assumes their leader's resurrection was imaginable. It assumes an individual bodily resurrection was an option for them.[111] It was not. This newly formulated belief in a bodily resurrection of Jesus literally sprang up overnight, thereby replacing thousands of years of core Jewish theology.

However, Dr. Robert Price argues in his book "Jesus is Dead," that resurrections are not all that astonishing from a first-century Jewish worldview.[112] He cites a passage in Mark 6:14-16 where King Herod said, "John, the man I beheaded, has been raised from the dead."[113] This response from Herod was in connection to an assumption from some that, "John the Baptist has been raised from the dead, and that is why miraculous powers are at work in him *(Jesus)*."[114] In response to Price, Dr. William Lane Craig points out,

> *Some have used the passage above to dispute the claim that the idea of an isolated resurrection in the midst of history was unknown in ancient Judaism. Such a response makes a category mistake... it is the confusion between revivification and resurrection. A person revived from death merely returned to the mortal life and would die again; a resurrection in Jewish thinking was to glory and immortality... So the Markan passage does not provide a counterexample to the claim that in Judaism resurrection was always a corporate, eschatological event, any more than does Jesus' reviving Lazarus from the grave.*[115]

---

[111] Timothy Keller, *The Reason for God* (New York, NY; Riverhead Books, 2008), 216.
[112] William L. Craig, accessed October 5, 2014, http://www.reasonablefaith.org/what-was-herod-thinking.
[113] The Holy Bible, New International Version (Grand Rapids, MI; Zondervan, 1984), Mark 6:16.
[114] Ibid. Mark 6:14. *(Jesus)* Italics added by the author.
[115] William L. Craig, accessed October 5, 2014, http://www.reasonablefaith.org/what-was-herod-thinking.

Simply put, this Markan passage is a reflection in a belief that the divine powers of John the Baptist were now transferred to Jesus. From Herod's perspective, "Jesus is John risen from the dead—not literally but figuratively."[116]

Liars Make Terrible Martyrs

The final difficulty to account for in the hallucination theory is the disciple's willingness to die for their testimony of a risen Jesus. Hallucinations have never, writes T.J. Thorburn, "stimulated people… to lead lives of the most rigid and consistent self-denial, and even suffering."[117] The only possible conclusion is the disciples truly saw the risen Jesus or they perpetrated the greatest deception in history and were willing to die for that deception. Some skeptics still hold to the latter. This hypothesis originally started in the midst of the 17th and 18th century where many European rationalists supported the notion that the disciples purposely deceived the masses so the cause of Jesus could continue.[118]

However, this supposed deception argument forces a conclusion that these early disciples were responsible for their own deaths and subsequently liable for the deaths of their closest family and friends. The disciples would have personally known

---

[116] Ibid.
[117] Josh McDowell, *The New Evidence That Demands a Verdict* (Nashville, TN; Thomas Nelson, 1999), 279.
[118] William L. Craig, accessed October 5, 2014, http://www.reasonablefaith.org/defenders-2-podcast/transcript/s6-17.

they were responsible due to this proposed "deceptive" belief in a resurrected Jesus. This theory lacks any psychological credibility and was essentially deserted by the 20th century. The only logical conclusion is to agree with the 19th century skeptic, David Strauss: "The historian must acknowledge that the disciples firmly believed that Jesus was risen."[119]

Finally, it is one thing to die for what one believes to be true but is actually a lie. However, it is quite another thing to die for what one knows to be a lie. Rational people are not willing to die for a known lie. The disciples and early followers were in an extraordinary position to know for certain if Jesus' resurrection was a known lie or the truth. Logic dictates they believed it to be true and history teaches us they were indeed rational.

Concluding Thoughts

Having considered the support from modern psychology and known historical facts, the hallucination theory simply does not stand. The evidence for a bodily resurrection of Jesus is strong and it is reasonable to believe that God raised Him from the dead. We live in a brilliant world full of wonder, enchantment, and awe. It is a place where miracles still happen. I freely concede that it is problematic for many in the Western world to embrace the reality of the miraculous. The difficulty rests on a focus toward empirical data coupled with an emphasis toward skepticism. However, for one wishing to expand their mind and appreciate the miraculous

---

[119] Josh McDowell, *The New Evidence That Demands a Verdict* (Nashville, TN; Thomas Nelson, 1999), 270.

work of God around the world, there is ample evidence from multiple sources indicated God's hand at work still today. For those daring enough to investigate, it seems to me, they will not be disappointed.

Having made this point however, even though people are physically healed, finances restored, relationships mended, and numerous other ways in which God moves, the biggest miracle is a translation from the knowledge of the resurrection event to a personal understanding of what that event can do for you. Because Jesus rose from the dead, there is hope all will be raised echoing Paul's words to the Corinthians, "…in Christ all will be made alive."[120] I encourage you to walk confidently in the truth that, "your faith" in the resurrection of Jesus is not "futile."[121]

---

[120] The Holy Bible, New International Version (Grand Rapids, MI; Zondervan, 1984), I Corinthians 15:22.
[121] Ibid. 15:17.

T.K. Anderson

CHAPTER FOUR
Jesus and Pagan Myths

Was Jesus Invented?

Some skeptics, although a minority position among scholars today, hold a view that Jesus never existed. One foundational aspect of this view is alleged similarities or parallels between Jesus and other deity figures such as Horus, Osiris, Mithras, and Dionysus. It is argued, therefore, these supposed parallels inspired the gospel writers to manufacture or invent the life of Jesus as represented in the Bible. Although Christianity may have mythical comparisons to pagan religions, there is no evidence to conclude Jesus was invented from prior pagan mythology or residual mystery religions. In truth, spurious endeavors from those who propagate the Christ myth theory, in an attempt to connect Jesus to pagan myths, are void of any factual evidence.

In this chapter, I will explore three matters; the thoughts of C.S. Lewis regarding myth in general, how ancient pagan myths most certainly do not accurately parallel the historical person of Jesus, and the perspective of first-century Jews regarding their view of God and assimilation with ancient pagan myths.

The Christ myth theory projects a concept that Christianity is a borrowed religion from a collection of prior pagan belief systems or perhaps a conglomeration of first or second-century mystery religions. This position holds that ultimately Jesus was a myth in the same manner as all pagan gods and should carry no more authority or credibility than other imaginary gods from antiquity. Agnostic Bart Ehrman describes "Jesus mythicism" as follows: "In simpler terms, the historical Jesus did not exist. Or if he did, he had virtually nothing to do with the founding of Christianity."[122] Although Ehrman does not ascribe to this view, as a liberal New Testament historian, he is well aware of this view from a scholarly level. Skeptic Earl Doherty penned, "(it is) the theory that no historical Jesus worthy of the name existed, that Christianity began with a belief in a spiritual, mythical figure, that the Gospels are essentially allegory and fiction, and that no single identifiable person lay at the root of the Galilean preaching tradition."[123]

However, former priest and New Testament scholar turned skeptic, John Dominic Crossan writes, "That he (Jesus) was

---

[122] Bart Ehrman, *Did Jesus Exist?* (New York, NY: Harper Collins, 2012), 12.
[123] Earl Doherty, *Jesus: Neither God Nor Man.* (Ottawa, Canada: Age of Reason, 2009), 7-8.

crucified is as sure as anything historical can ever be, since both Josephus and Tacitus...agree with the Christian accounts on at least that basic fact."[124] Together with Crossan and Ehrman, there is wide scholarly consensus that the Christ myth theory is in fact outdated and not based in facts.[125] In order to propose a thoughtful response to those who may hold to this theory and in an attempt to lean toward an objective rather than subjective perspective, I would like to begin with a brief historical assessment regarding the Christ myth theory.

A Brief Assessment

In his influential book *The Case For The Real Jesus*, author Lee Strobel shares an interview with Dr. Edwin Yamauchi, referred to as "a scholar's scholar."[126] In discussing the theory, Strobel asks, "Who popularized the idea that Jesus' resurrection was derived from the worship of dying and rising fertility gods?"[127] Yamauchi responded,

> *In the scholarly world, these comparisons were promoted by a group of scholars called the Religionsgeschichtliche schule...That's the so-called History of Religions School, which flourished at the end of the nineteenth and into the early twentieth centuries. The seminal work by Richard Reitzenstein was published in German in 1910...He*

---

[124] John Dominic Crossan, *Jesus: A Revolutionary Biography.* (New York, NY: HarperOne 1995), 145.

[125] Mark W. Foreman, *Come Let Us Reason.* (Nashville, TN: B&H Publishing Group, 2012), 173. The *Religionsgeschichtliche Schule*, or history of religions school, coming out of Germany, was one of the instigators of this line of thinking, but was abandoned by the early 1930's because of its radical methodology and approach. See Kurt Rudolph, "Religionsgeschichtliche Schule," The Encyclopedia of Religion, ed. Mircea Eliade (New York: Macmillan, 1987), 12:293-96.

[126] John E. Wineland, ed., *The Light of Discovery.* (Eugene, OR: Pickwick, 2007), xiii.

[127] Lee Strobel, *The Case For The Real Jesus.* (New York, NY: Zondervan, 2007), 166.

> *thought the sacrifice of Christ aligned itself with the killing of a bull by Mithras. Carsten Colpe and others severely criticized the anachronistic use of sources by these scholars. On the popular level, Sir James Frazer gathered a mass of parallels in his multivolume work called The Golden Bough, which was published in 1906. He discussed Osiris of Egypt, Adonis of Syria, Attis of Asia Minor, and Tammuz of Mesopotamia, and concluded there was a common rising and dying fertility god. Unfortunately, much of his work was based on a misreading of the evidence, but nevertheless this helped introduce these ideas to the popular culture. Later, in the 1930's, three influential French scholars claimed that Christianity was influenced by the Hellenistic mystery religions…there was a widespread view that there was a general, common mystery religion, but upon a closer examination of the sources, nobody believes that any longer…In fact, by the mid-twentieth century, scholars had established that the sources used in these writings were far from satisfactory and the parallels were much too superficial. It was pretty much of a closed issue in the scholarly community.*[128]

Mark W. Foreman, Ph.D. agrees with Yamauchi's assessment both with the origin of the theory and ultimate rejection from a scholarly level. Foreman writes, "The copycat theory emerged in the mid-nineteenth century and was popularized mostly through James Frazer's *The Golden Bough* (1890). It continued until the early twentieth century, when its methods and conclusion were rejected by critical scholars."[129] Even though conservative and liberal scholars have universally rejected the theory, it is also true, that this belief has experienced a type of

---
[128] Ibid, 166-167.
[129] Mark W. Foreman, *Come Let Us Reason*. (Nashville, TN: B&H Publishing Group, 2012), 172.

resurrection at the popular level. This time exists inside the world of YouTube videos, blogs, and endless comment sections amid social media sites. There seems to be something inside the human psyche, which stirs our imagination and seeks to provide answers to the things that are mysterious. A type of cerebral cloudiness caught somewhere between postmodern philosophy and pre-renaissance mystical enchantment. In an effort to sift through the cloudiness, I would like to circle back to those three matters mentioned earlier.

C.S. Lewis and Myth

Now that I have set the foundation regarding this theory and given history of its origin, I would like to pivot the discussion by seeking help from one of the twentieth century's intellectual giants, C.S. Lewis. Lewis can be of great service to us on account of his struggle with this very ideology. Prior to his conversion to Christianity, Lewis struggled with the idea of Christianity being immune from mythical scrutiny. It seems to me his thoughts on the subject matter can be of assistance. Lewis wrote,

> *"The accepted position seemed to be that religions were normally a mere farrago of nonsense, though our own, by a fortunate exception, was exactly true...But on what grounds could I believe in this exception? It obviously was in some general sense the same kind of thing as all the rest. Why was it so differently treated? Need I, at any rate, continue to treat it differently? I was very anxious not to."[130]*

---

[130] C.S. Lewis, *Surprised by Joy.* (New York: NY, Harcourt Brace, 1988), 62-63.

Lewis details his spiritual journey in *Surprised by Joy*. In it, he describes the early years of his life up to his change of heart and mind on a "drive to Whipsnade one sunny morning. When we set out I did not believe that Jesus Christ is the Son of God, and when we reached the zoo I did."[131] It would be sophomoric at best and intellectually dishonest at worst to simply brush over this event in Lewis' life. This moment was not a flash point type occurrence, "nor" an outbreak, "in great emotion."[132] Lewis wrote, "It was more like when a man, after long sleep, still lying motionless in bed, becomes aware that he is now awake."[133] From that fundamental moment in 1931, Lewis turned his gift of intellectual proficiency and literary brilliance into a powerful voice of influence for the Christian faith. It was not until, however, Lewis conquered his own perspective regarding the Christ myth theory.

In a 1916 letter to his friend Arthur Greeves, "All religions," Lewis wrote, "are merely man's invention."[134] He continued in the letter to assert, "Often too, great men were regarded as gods after their death – such as Heracles or Odin: thus after the death of a Hebrew philosopher Yeshua (whose name we have corrupted into Jesus) he became regarded as a god, a cult sprang up…Christianity came into being."[135]

It was from this mindset that Lewis "went to Oxford and

---

[131] C.S. Lewis, *Surprised by Joy*. (New York, NY: Harcourt Brace, 1988), 237.
[132] Ibid, 237.
[133] Ibid, 237.
[134] Art Lindsley, *C.S. Lewis's Case For Christ*. (Downers Grove, IL: IVP Books, 2005), 68.
[135] Ibid, 68.

later was given a position on the faculty."[136] While teaching at Oxford, in the late 1920's, Lewis describes a moment when he, J.R.R. Tolkien, and Hugo Dyson "were having dinner at Magdalen College."[137] During dinner, Lewis shared with Tolkien the difficulty regarding Jesus and the connection to pagan myths. Lewis held that "myths are lies."[138]

Therefore, under Lewis's view, the story of Christ, which Tolkien also viewed as myth, would be untrue. Tolkien shared with Lewis his perspective, and the discussion lasted "almost all night, during which they walked around Oxford and talked through this issue."[139] Departing from this instrumental dialogue and throughout the ensuing years, Lewis developed a resourceful and impactful viewpoint on the matter. Contrary to his former beliefs, Lewis developed the idea that myth in general may contain an element of untruth or errors, but the same myth does hold a portion of God's reality.

Through this perspective, Lewis removed the stinging effect of the negative implication regarding parallel myth stories. If I remove the bullet from the gun, what harm remains, but to toss it? But even a toss would leave only but a mark. The fear of death has been disconnected from the device. Even more so, Lewis takes this consideration much deeper.

---
[136] Ibid, 68.
[137] Ibid, 69.
[138] Ibid. 69.
[139] Ibid, 69.

Common Themes

Since, as Lewis held, we are "sub-creators," we have the ability to invent mythic stories fundamental to our experience as human beings. On account of this creative ability, it would not be a surprise to find connections or similarities among common stories. If indeed "myths are splintered fragments of the true light," [140] one may conclude an underlying connection, a comparable literary arrow pointing, directing to a greater truth. Tolkien, who initially introduced Lewis to this line of reasoning once wrote, "I believe that legends and myths are largely made of truth, and indeed present aspects of it can only be perceived in this mode; and long ago certain truths and modes of this kind were discovered and must always appear."[141]

It is a difficult task indeed to mount a suitable argument in contradiction to this view. The skeptic could respond, "You are inferring a god figure," to which Lewis and Tolkien would most expectedly reply, "Exactly, so let us discuss the idea of God and why we conclude there are good reasons for His existence. Thus showing, God infusing a literary device within the stories of mankind directing us back to Himself."

The True Myth

Lewis ultimately argued the story of Jesus is the true myth. As he studied with more intense scrutiny the Gospel stories and the writings of those responsible for the content, Lewis concluded,

---

[140] Ibid, 69.
[141] J.R.R. Tolkien, ltr 31 in *The Letters of J.R.R. Tolkien*, (New York, NY: Houghton Mifflin, 1981), 147.

"I was by now too experienced in literary criticism to regard the Gospels as myths. They had not the mythical taste."[142] As an expert in medieval literature and additionally possessing the uncanny talent for writing fascinating mythic stories, Lewis was able to sense the difference between the Gospels and other myths. In a later letter to Arthur Greeves, Lewis wrote, "The story of Christ is simply a true myth: a myth working on us in the same way as others, but with this tremendous difference that it really happened."[143]

Lewis concluded instead of Christ standing in opposition to the mythic stories of old, Christ stands in fulfillment of what those stories were unable to realize. Literally, Christ stands as a historical fulfillment of the ancient's inner yearnings. For in Christ, we see truth, justice, love, forgiveness, eternity, and miracles complete; as if Jesus, "came not to put an end to myth but to take all that is most essential in the myth up into himself and make it real."[144]

Pagan Myths Fail

Even though Lewis developed a unique case diffusing the parallel stories argument, a second matter to consider is how pagan myths actually fail to truly parallel Jesus. The proponents of

---

[142] C.S. Lewis, *Surprised by Joy*. (New York, NY: Harcourt Brace, 1988), 236.
[143] C.S. Lewis, *Letters of C.S. Lewis*. (New York, NY: Harcourt Brace, 1988), 288.
[144] Louis A. Markos, "Myth Matters Why C.S. Lewis's books remain models for Christian apologists in the 21st century." *Christianity Today The Magazine*, April 23, 2001, accessed July 3, 2016, http://www.christianitytoday.com/ct/2001/april23/1.32.html.

the Christ myth theory claim that Jesus is a fictitious person. They claim biblical writers utilized a patch quilt of ancient stories to create the character. Leaving behind the obvious main problem for a moment, that of Jesus needing to not exist in order for this theory to stand, I wish to tackle the inherent conflicts of the supposed parallels.

The most simplified version of the theory can be viewed on a widespread YouTube video entitled *Zeitgeist*. The primary source for the documentary comes from writer Dorothy M. Murdock. In the movie, it is claimed that Jesus shares the same virgin birth, same birthday, divine titles, birth location, miracle-working power, crucifixion, resurrection, disciple count, and overall general biography with numerous other former god figures. This tactic is called parallelism. Mark W. Foreman writes,

> *"This tactic of citing parallels is not new. In fact, in a 1962 article in the Journal of Biblical Literature, Samuel Sandmel referred to such sloppy scholarship as "parallelomania," which he defined as "that extravagance among scholars which first overdoes the supposed similarity in passages and then proceeds to describe source and derivation as if implying literary connection flowing in an inevitable or predetermined direction." Zeitgeist is parallelomania on steroids."*[145]

Virgin Birth

Starting with the virgin birth claim, upon inspection, we

---

[145] Mark W. Foreman, *Come Let Us Reason.* (Nashville, TN: B&H Publishing Group, 2012), 172.

find the following: Mithras was born out of a rock, the mother of Horus was the wife of Osiris, the mother of Attis conceived when a pomegranate dropped in her lap, and the mother of Krishna had seven children prior to his birth. There simply is no comparison with the biblical writers' description of Mary and the virgin birth story of Jesus. Strobel's interview from earlier continued on this very topic,

> *I pulled out a list of parallels between Jesus and Mithras. "First, popular writers claim that Mithras was born of a virgin," I said. "Is that true that this was what Mithraism taught?" Yamauchi looked pained. "No, that's definitely not true," he insisted. "He was born out of a rock." "A rock?" "Yes, the rock birth is commonly depicted in Mithraic reliefs," he explained. "Mithras emerges fully grown and naked except for a Phrygian cap, and he's holding a dagger and torch. In some variations, flames shoot out from the rock, or he's holding a globe in his hand." I chuckled. "So unless the rock is considered a virgin, this parallel with Jesus evaporates," I said. "Entirely correct," he said. "And that means he wasn't born in a cave, which some writers claim is a second parallel to Christianity."[146]*

Crucifixion

How about the crucifixion accounts? Were former mythic figures crucified like Jesus or are their mythical deaths of a different sort? Upon examination, we find Krishna died from wounds inflicted by an arrow shot to the foot. Attis died in the wilderness shortly after he castrated himself. Horus was most

---

[146] Lee Strobel, *The Case For The Real Jesus.* (New York, NY: Zondervan, 2007), 170-171.

likely stung by a scorpion, but has two death stories neither, relating to a crucifixion. Adonis was killed by a wild boar. Even Murdock admits,

> *"When it is asserted that Horus (or Osiris) was "crucified" it should be kept in mind that it was not part of the Horus/Osiris myth that the murdered god was held down and nailed on a cross...However, Egyptian deities, including Horus, were depicted in cruciform with arms extended or outstretched, as in various images that are comparable to crucifixes."*[147]

Foreman rebuts, "So, according to Murdock, anytime deities are depicted with arms outstretched, we are justified in claiming they were crucified."[148]

Dying and Rising Gods

What about the similarities of dying and rising gods? Surely, this shows Jesus as an invented myth based upon analogous stories. This claim is reminiscent of the popular similarities between John F. Kennedy and Abraham Lincoln that actually show no causal connection. For example: Kennedy was elected in 1960 and Lincoln was elected in 1860, Kennedy and Lincoln each have seven letters in their names, Kennedy had a secretary named Lincoln and Lincoln had a secretary named Kennedy, both presidents were assassinated on a Friday and shot in the back of the head, both presidents were succeeded by vice presidents named Johnson. These similarities serve to prove that it

---

[147] Mark W. Foreman, *Come Let Us Reason*. (Nashville, TN: B&H Publishing Group, 2012), 178-179.
[148] Ibid, 179.

is easy to collect any number of insignificant facts or data points and then claim a connection. It is sensible to conclude, however, that similarities among religions does not equate to dependence upon other religions. Correlation does not equal causation. Foreman concludes, "Christ died for the sins of mankind; none of the pagan gods died for someone else. Pagan gods died under compulsion, but Jesus died willingly. Jesus died and was raised once; the pagan gods die cyclically…His death and resurrection were actual events of history."[149]

Birthdays and Mangers

In a final attempt to bolster the Christ myth theory, the promoters of this theory submit two strange parallels that have no basis in actual fact: a December 25th birthday and a manger visit from three kings. However, the Bible does not mention a birth date for Jesus: in truth, we do not know what day He was born. The Bible is simply silent on the topic. Additionally, the Bible does not mention how many magi came to visit Jesus and it would be wild speculation to assume it was three within the first weeks of His birth. Foreman labels this the *non-biblical fallacy*. Beyond this fallacy, the most concerning foundational element of the Christ myth theory is simply the source material. Historically, there are almost no primary sources prior to the time of Christ. Most literature regarding the mythic stories is from post first-century Christianity. A better argument can be made that, th theory is simply the source material. Historically, there arGnostics who took

---

[149] Mark W. Foreman, *Come Let Us Reason.* (Nashville, TN: B&H Publishing Group, 2012), 183.

up Christian ideas.r[150]

A First Century Mindset

Finally, the last matter to consider in dismissing the Christ myth theory is that of properly understanding the mindset of first-century Judaism. In order to hold to the Christ myth theory, one would need to show how pagan myths could have infiltrated the teachings of the Gospel writers. There are two reasons why this would be a difficult case to substantiate. First, Bruce Metzger points out,

> *"Unlike other countries bordering the Mediterranean Sea, Palestine has been extremely barren in yielding archaeological remains of the paraphernalia and places of worship connected with Mysteries. One second-century source that contains a detailed list of places where Isis was worshipped: 67 in Egypt and 55 outside Egypt, only one of which is in Palestine – namely, Strato's Tower in Caesarea, which was built by the wicked king Herod."*[151]

There is simply no archeological or historical data to support the claim that ancient mystery religions were intermixed within first-century Judaism. In truth, Roman multi-god worship represented the antithesis of the Jewish thought. Historical evidence clearly indicates the Jews "deeply resented the signs of pagan culture in

---

[150] Alister E. McGrath, *Intellectuals Don't Need God*. (Grand Rapids, MI: Zondervan, 1992), 121.
[151] Mark W. Foreman, *Come Let Us Reason*. (Nashville, TN: B&H Publishing Group, 2012), 175.

their ancient homeland."[152] They resisted Rome to the point of Jerusalem's destruction in A.D. 70.

Exclusively Monotheistic

The second point rests in the fact that, "Judaism was an extremely exclusive monotheistic religion and would not have tolerated the syncretism of the mystery religions. Christianity posed even more exclusivity and has often been referred to as the "anti-mystery" religion." [153] Christianity was founded on a historical figure that carried a new message of hope, love, forgiveness, and eternal life for all mankind. In their minds, Jesus was the fulfillment of Jewish Old Testament prophecies. Early Christians were rooted in Old Testament law not mythic rituals or pagan thoughts. Christianity was a different message but did not allow the incorporation of pagan customs or teachings. This stands in contradiction to the mystery religions, which were very inclusive.

In the mystery religions, first-century adherents could worship the emperor and still hold to the worship of their pagan gods. Conversely, early Christians were persecuted because they resisted foreign teachings from infiltrating their message. In non-Christian sources, we find this point to be true. Pliny, the governor of Bithynia in 112 AD, wrote to the Emperor Trajan, "In it he expressed his dismay over the rapid spread of the Christian faith.

---

[152] Bruce L. Shelley, *Church History In Plain Language 4th Ed*, (Nashville, TN: Thomas Nelson, 2013), 5.
[153] Mark W. Foreman, *Come Let Us Reason*. (Nashville, TN: B&H Publishing Group, 2012), 175.

Pliny was afraid that the shrines of the pagan gods would soon be completely deserted."[154] The book of Acts echoes this same worry led by a Silversmith named Demetrius. He was a craftsman in Ephesus and was not pleased with Paul, Gaius, or Aristarchus. The followers of Jesus were converting Ephesians away from pagan gods. The Ephesian tradesman proclaimed, "This fellow Paul has convinced and led astray large numbers of people here in Ephesus and in practically the whole province of Asia. He says that man-made gods are no gods at all. There is danger not only that our trade will lose its good name, but also that the temple of the great goddess Artemis will be discredited."[155]

Acts records another incident where the people of Lystra worshiped Paul and Barnabas. "The gods have come down to us in human form!"[156] They thought Paul was Zeus and Barnabas was Hermes. Paul rebuked them and said, "Men, why are you doing this? We too are only men, human like you. We are bringing you good news, telling you to turn from these worthless things to the living God."[157] These biblical accounts confirm the early followers of Jesus had no desire to mix religious beliefs with their message.

Concluding Thoughts

Indeed, while Christianity has some pagan or mystical comparisons, Christianity was not inspired by pagan mythology or by the mystery religions of the first or second centuries. The

---

[154] Bruce L. Shelley, *Church History In Plain Language 4th Ed*, (Nashville, TN: Thomas Nelson, 2013), 33.
[155] The Holy Bible, NIV Translation, (Grand Rapids, MI: Zondervan, 1984), Acts 19:26-27.
[156] Ibid, Acts 14:11.
[157] Ibid, Acts 14:15.

writings of C.S. Lewis clarify the idea of the Gospel of Jesus as The True Myth. For in the story of Christ, all mythic literary elements are fulfilled. Lewis comes to this conclusion because in the Gospels, we have both the story and the history. Skillfully, Lewis's unique approach removes the discussion of authenticating or refuting the parallel myth stories.

However, even when the story of Christ is compared alongside the supposed parallels, the supporters of the Christ myth theory fall short. From the comparative accounts of the virgin birth, crucifixion, and resurrection, to the magi and birthday invention, the parallels simply are not there. Lastly, sustained with a firm understanding that first century Judaism was incongruent with mythic stories and pagan rituals, the idea of Gospel writers plagiarizing pagan myths to create a fictitious Jesus account is beyond reason. Therefore, it is reasonable to conclude that the Christ myth theory remains false.

CHAPTER FIVE
Transposition

Is There More To This Natural World?

If one was to take a summary of important theological questions, it is clear that some questions require more consideration than others. One such question that has consumed my attention from time to time is, how do I know if my spiritual experiences are not mistaken inferences derived by my natural inclinations? In other words, is there a supernatural or metaphysical world that intersects my natural, physical world? Are my mind and body separate? I want to believe there is a supernatural world, due to my Christian principles and my desire for an afterlife, hope on earth, peace with men, and ultimate justice. Additionally, from a young age, I have felt as though my encounters with God have been strong and impactful spiritual phenomena. Within the deepest well of my being, there is something genuinely real about those experiences and how I have interpreted them. But am I wrong?

Skeptics hold a viewpoint, and argue eloquently I might add, from a perspective that only a natural world exists, and there is no good evidence or exemplary data to conclude otherwise. Freud's perspective was that "Religion is comparable to a childhood neurosis"[158] and "Religion is an illusion and it derives its strength from the fact that it falls in with our instinctual desires."[159] Consequently, for many, this is a deep question and warrants robust consideration combined with thoughtful answers.

Recently, I have re-experienced a useful viewpoint from C.S. Lewis. Even though the supernatural world looks like the natural world, we can be very confident there exists a spiritual source to the phenomenon embedded within our natural human experiences. Utilizing Lewis's concept of Transposition, I will set out to show that there is a strong basis for our natural world consisting of more than purely natural forces.

A Spiritual Intersection

Lewis begins his essay on Transposition with an illustration describing the spiritual experience of speaking in tongues as found in the biblical account of Acts, Chapter Two. I

---

[158] Kendra Cherry, *Freud and Religion*, accessed June 30, 2016, https://www.verywell.com/freud-religion-2795858.
[159] Ibid.

found this to be a fascinating illustration coming from Lewis who admittedly struggled with the phenomenon, as an "embarrassing phenomenon."[160] However, I believe it serves as a full-bodied illustration for the inquiry. The term for speaking in tongues is *glossolalia* and is constructed from the Greek words *glossa*, meaning, "tongue" or "language" and *laleo*, meaning, "to speak, talk, chat." The term has been used to describe an extraordinary linguistic phenomenon individuals experience in relation to what they believe to be the spiritual realm intersecting with their natural world. Without needing to wander into a theological discussion on the merits of this experience, if in fact it is true, it is sufficient to say for the sake of this discussion, this phenomenon serves to illustrate a very clear example between the interaction of heavenly and earthly realms.

The skeptic will quickly point out the most likely explanation for this experience is hysteria and there are no grounds to hypothesize anything but the cause being derived from the human mind. With this example and most all spiritual examples, Lewis writes,

> *Put in its most general terms our problem is that of the obvious continuity between things which are admittedly natural and things which, it is claimed, are spiritual; the reappearance in what professes to be our supernatural life of all the same old elements which make up our natural life and (it would seem) of no others. If we have really been visited by a revelation from beyond Nature, is it not*

---

[160] C.S. Lewis, *Weight of Glory* (New York, NY: HarperOne, 1949), 91.

> *very strange that an Apocalypse can furnish heaven with nothing more than selections from terrestrial experience (crowns, thrones, and music), that devotion can find no language but that of human lovers, and that the rite whereby Christians enact a mystical union should turn out to be only the old, familiar act of eating and drinking?*[161]

An Adaptation

It would do us well to pivot to the concept from Lewis' essay called Transposition. When I use the word Transposition, I mean an "adaptation from a richer to poorer medium."[162] We can all relate to this concept through a few simple illustrations. I borrow from Lewis the following ideas.

If we were to transpose an original orchestra score to a singular piano sheet, it would be reduced from the conductor's higher form to a lower form of just one instrument. If we were to consider the same type of feeling we experience as butterflies in the pit of our stomach from love, guilt, fear, or loss, we can understand the emotional differences within our human experiences, yet the physical demonstration of those differing emotions is the same. If we were to talk of tears of joy or tears of sadness, we can illustrate that our physical body displays the same outcome yet is driven from a higher form from within us that is truly experiencing the phenomenon of emotion.

As humans, we experience the idea of Transposition in our everyday life. The concept here is that, we find "our emotional life

---
[161] Ibid, 94.
[162] Ibid, 99.

to be higher than the life of our sensations – not, of course, morally higher, but richer, more varied, more subtle."[163] We are prone to make a simple mistake of equating a one-for-one correspondence between two systems. Even the most ardent skeptic would agree it is not always true that X in one system must represent X in the other system. Lewis points out, "There never could be correspondence of that sort where the one system was really richer than the other."[164] It seems to me the correspondence between human emotions and human senses is a good example of the idea of "adaptation from a richer to poorer medium."[165]

Understanding a Higher Form

From here, we ought to consider the following; the only true way for the lower form to understand the higher form would be to truly understand the higher form. In the case of the orchestra to piano Transposition, the only way we can understand and appreciate the original score is if and only if we understand there are more instruments in the world than just pianos. If we only know of pianos, then we have no context or concept of how the original score rightly sounds. We are limited in our understanding and actually have no knowledge of what we are missing. Furthermore, we are not aware of the limitation until and only if we discover, by some means, the truth of the existence of other instruments. It would be a most sad condition to endure, and yet not capable of understanding the sadness of the state.

---

[163] C.S. Lewis, *Weight of Glory* (New York, NY: HarperOne, 1949), 98.
[164] Ibid, 99.
[165] Ibid, 99.

Imagine the following, you are attempting to communicate with a creature who lives in a two-dimensional world. His life consists of lines on a sheet of paper, yet from your three-dimensional world you attempt to describe and draw out for your friend the beauty and joy of your other world. Let us assume he can hear you, yet is still limited by the conceptual limitations of two dimensions. Would not your new friend continue to object with you every time you shared how the lines on the paper are a cube, yet he only sees lines? The impasse is found in that he is unable to conceive of the idea of a cube. He may respond, "A square yes, but a cube that is mysterious and who can know of such things?" Lewis writes of the interaction like this,

> *You keep on telling me of this other world and its unimaginable shapes which you call solid. But isn't it very suspicious that all the shapes which you offer me as images or reflections of the solid ones turn out on inspection to be simply the old two-dimensional shapes of my own world as I have always known it? Is it not obvious that your vaunted other world, so far from being the archetype, is a dream which borrows all its elements from this one?*[166]

We now can resolve if the supernatural is higher than the natural, which by nature of the descriptions it would be, then we would expect the inhabitants of the natural world to have difficulty understanding the supernatural. The skeptic is fulfilling his role in asserting he does not understand or see the higher form. He would be unable to, until and unless, he is able to view the natural realm

---

[166] C.S. Lewis, *Weight of Glory* (New York, NY: HarperOne, 1949), 101.

from the supernatural realm. It would be useless to ridicule or demean the skeptic for approaching a Transposition from the lower form. As he observes the evidence in front of him, the conclusion can only be what he perceives.

The Switch

However, everything changes when we switch the approach. When we approach the Transposition from above, we have new perspective and we receive new understanding. This new view is not limited to the supernatural and natural discussion. This new viewpoint finds its way within our human emotion and sense consideration, as well as with the Flatlander, and our piano player. When we look from above, the perspective changes and the concept of Transposition takes hold. How do I best describe this? It is, "as if the picture knew enough of the three-dimensional world to be aware that it was flat."[167]

Meaning

We can now shift to the idea of meaning. The last bastion of hope for the skeptic is to hold a theoretical perspective based solely on facts and denies meaning. The foundation for the critic is supported "in the words 'merely' or 'nothing but.'"[168] The critic observes every detail yet blocks any meaning attached to the experience. But the mistake of the critic is failing to see "there is

---
[167] Ibid, 106.
[168] Ibid, 113.

nothing else there; except meaning."[169] Consider for a moment the life and experience of my dog. When I use my finger to point to a treat, my dog does not essentially understand that I am actually pointing. He does not understand that my finger serves as a marker or a symbol of something else. He simply sniffs my finger and waits for his treat as he frantically begins the hunt for his prize. His life is devoid of actual meaning.

We cannot prevent the critic from holding this viewpoint and refusing to see things from the higher form, but we are not prevented from encouraging the skeptic to leave the life of an animal and discover this higher form. Toward the end of his essay, Lewis concludes,

> *In a period when factual realism is dominant we shall find people deliberately inducing upon themselves this doglike mind. A man who has experienced love from within will deliberately go about to inspect it analytically from outside and regard the results of this analysis as truer than his experience. The extreme limit of this self-blinding is seen in those who, like the rest of us, have consciousness, yet go about to study the human organism as if they did not know it was conscious.*[170]

If we approach the skeptic's mindset critically however, we will find the cynic falls upon his own sword. The very consciousness he denies is utilized to deny its existence. Here we end in a circular argument much like a dog chasing his tail.

---

[169] Ibid, 114.
[170] Ibid, 114.

Final Thoughts

In addition to the thoughts borrowed from Lewis, we have further suggestions to reinforce our case. In the aforementioned case of speaking in tongues, contemporary research from neuroscientist Dr. Andrew Newberg shows a different part of the brain becoming activated during the experience. Newberg writes, "When I compared the scans of five Pentecostal women speaking in tongues…I saw significant differences."[171] He dedicates an entire chapter to his findings in his 2006 book, *Born To Believe.*

It seems to me, this points to a connection with how the brain responds from a lower form to what the participants are claiming they experience in a higher form. With additional study, Newberg and other researchers are attempting to validate Near-Death Experiences as well. Combine this with Dr. Craig Keener's ground breaking two-volume set entitled *Miracles* alongside Dr. J.P. Moreland's *The Soul: How We Know It's Real and Why It Matters,* and we can see a cumulative effect based upon solid philosophy strengthened with facts plus experience. In the final analysis, we have solid reasons to believe in a supernatural world intersecting with our natural world.

---

[171] Andrew Newberg, *Born To Believe* (New York, NY: Free Press, 2006), 200.

CHAPTER SIX
God's Non-Binding Agreement

The Law of Christ Fulfills The Law of Moses

An imposing subject indeed is the discussion of the connection and interaction between two deeply entrenched theological topics, Law and Gospel. As the body of Christ continues this dialogue, we can celebrate our diversity of thought as the center of our discussion remains upon Christ and His salvific work. Does the Law of Moses apply to my Christian experience today? Are we required to keep the Sabbath? What about the other nine commandments? Because of grace, are we free as Christians to do whatever we want?

These are the types of questions to be resolved as we discover the relationship between the Law and Gospel. I stand in agreement with the words of Wayne Strickland: "It is imperative and helpful to decide the proper relationship of Mosaic Law to the saint."[172] I will argue in this chapter that the application of Mosaic Law to the life of the Christian is not binding as being under the Law, instead, as followers of Jesus, we are unreservedly under the Law of Christ (1 Corinthians 9:21).

If we begin our inquiry from the perspective of heaven, we can see the interaction between God and humanity from a top-down view. This view allows us to see that, as the Psalmist writes, "Blessed is the nation whose God is Yahweh, the people He chose for His inheritance" (Psalm 33:12). The blessings and plan of God for humanity was determined by Yahweh to transport through the blessed people we now know as Israel. Baylis writes,

> *According to Exodus 6:6-8, there are three stages for God's gracious action as Yahweh. The first stage, deliverance from Egypt, is complete, and the third stage is yet to come: possession of the land promised to Abraham. At Sinai, stage two has arrived: "I will take you as my own people, and I will be your God." The Law is not a bogus door prize. It is the opportunity of a lifetime. These people are about to become the people of God. They have been chosen to enter into a covenant with God in which Yahweh commits himself to them as his people and they recognize Yahweh as their God.*[173]

---

[172] Stanley N. Gundry, *Five Views on Law and Gospel* (Grand Rapids, MI: Zondervan, 1999), 9.
[173] Albert H. Baylis, *From Creation to the Cross* (Grand Rapids, MI: Zondervan, 1996), 122.

This outpouring of God's blessing to the people of Israel was on no account of their own. This was not a works-based blessing, but rather an outpouring and continuation of God's promise found in the Abrahamic covenant (Genesis 12:1-3; Genesis 15:18-21). The goal of Yahweh was to have His presence with His people (Exodus 29:43). He says, "I will dwell among the Israelites and be their God. They will know that I am Yahweh their God, who brought them out of Egypt so that I might dwell among them" (Exodus 29:45-46). At Sinai, Israel entered into a covenant with God through the Mosaic Law. It was the law that ultimately pointed the way to Christ (Galatians 3:24).

The Mosaic Law

In his writings, Douglas J. Moo points out that the Mosaic Law "was never intended to be, and could never in fact be, a means of salvation."[174] He continues to describe the Mosaic Law as holding three purposes. The first was for God to "reveal his character to the people of Israel and demand that the people conform to it."[175] Moo continues in this line of thought, "The Mosaic law is not *simply* revelation of God's character; it is demand for conformity to that character . . .What we are insisting on here is that the Mosaic law is, indeed, law."[176] Additionally, some of the laws directly point to God's character. For instance, "we are not to murder because God reverences and sanctifies

---

[174] Stanley N. Gundry, *Five Views on Law and Gospel* (Grand Rapids, MI: Zondervan, 1999), 324.
[175] Ibid, 324.
[176] Ibid, 335.

human life."[177] Indirectly, the law, by way of dietary restrictions, shows the people of God should separate and set themselves apart for a holy purpose just as God is holy and separate. More specifically, "the sacrificial laws teach still another truth about God, that he cannot tolerate sin without some kind of shedding of blood to compensate for that sin."[178]

Three Segments

At this point, some theological positions based upon the Covenant and Evangelical perspectives divide the differing laws into three segments. VanGemeren writes, "The laws of the Old Testament have also been commonly categorized as moral, ceremonial, and civil. Each one of the Ten Commandments expresses the moral law of God, whereas most laws in the Pentateuch regulate the rituals and ceremonies (ceremonial laws) and the civil life of Israel as a nation (civil laws)."[179]

Kaiser opines, "There are some misconceptions concerning the law that are often marshaled in opposition to the Christian use of the law as just described."[180] Moo references this line of thinking by further explaining, "The moral commandments, it is assumed, are eternally binding in the form in which they were originally given, while the ceremonial and the civil ones, finding their fulfillment in Christ, cease to act as immediate guides to Christian behavior."[181]

---

[177] Ibid, 336.
[178] Ibid, 336.
[179] Ibid, 30.
[180] Ibid, 188.
[181] Ibid, 336.

This form of triadic description concerning Mosaic Law is essential to the theological viewpoints disagreeing with the thesis of this chapter. For their theological premise to stand, a continuity of the law must apply from the Old Testament into the New Testament, whereas we hold that there is a discontinuity in that "the entire Mosaic law comes to fulfillment in Christ, and this fulfillment means that this law is no longer a direct and immediate source of, or judge of, the conduct of God's people. Christian behavior, rather, is now guided directly by the law of Christ."[182]

Difficulty with Continuity

One difficulty with holding to the continuity perspective is what to do with certain commandments within the Decalogue. It is difficult to distinguish how the moral or eternal value, for instance, of the command to honor your mother and father, "so that you may live long in the land the Lord your God is giving you" (Exodus 20:12) carries continuity "when Paul reapplies this commandment to his Christian reader (Ephesians 6:2-3), he universalizes the promise: 'that it may go well with you and that you may enjoy long life on the earth.'"[183] Another challenging eternal moral law dilemma rests in the commandment to honor the Sabbath. Moreover, Moo continues, "Jews in Jesus' and Paul's day certainly did not divide up the law into categories; on the contrary, there was a strong insistence that the law was a unity and could not be obeyed in parts."[184] The burden of exegetical proof

---

[182] Ibid, 343.
[183] Ibid, 337.
[184] Ibid, 337.

lies in the court of those who claim the Mosaic Law can be divided into differing segments.

New Testament

The New Testament does not show the law being applied "to only one part of the law."[185] Additionally, Paul writes in his letter to the Galatians that we are not privileged to pick and choose what parts of the law we want to keep, "I declare to every man who lets himself be circumcised that he is obligated to obey the whole law" (Galatians 5:3). Likewise, James reminds us, "Whoever keeps the whole law and yet stumbles at just one point is guilty of breaking all of it" (James 2:10). Moo concludes, "These points suffice to show that the continuity of the law in the new covenant cannot be founded on such a distinction among the different 'kinds' of laws."[186]

Supervision Until Christ

The second purpose of Mosaic Law was, "to supervise Israel in the time before Christ."[187] Apart from the theological discussions regarding Mosaic Law, from a historical context, there is no argument that the nation of Israel was a distinct culture. The worship, dietary, and lifestyle components of the law served to preserve the people and set their nation apart for God's purposes. Correspondingly, the New Testament shows that the law served as a preserving mechanism to tutor the people until the arrival of Christ. In Galatians 3:24, it is stated, "the law was put in charge to

---

[185] Ibid, 337.
[186] Ibid, 337.
[187] Ibid, 324.

lead us to Christ." It is evident from Galatians 3:15-4:7 that Paul is referring to "the purpose of the law in the history of the people of Israel."[188] Moo comments, "The first person plural ('us') probably refers to Paul and his fellow Jews, not Paul and his fellow Christians."[189]

Furthermore, the key word *paidagogos*, "denoted a person, usually a servant, who had charge of young children. The ancient *pedagogue* was not a teacher but a babysitter. Galatians 3:24 is therefore asserting that the Mosaic Law functioned among the people of Israel to direct their behavior until the time of their maturity, when the promised Messiah would be revealed (cf. Galatians 4:1-7)."[190]

To Bring Knowledge of Sin

The third purpose of the Mosaic Law was "to imprison Israel and, by extension, all people under sin."[191] Paul writes in Romans 3:19-20; 7:7-12 that the law is designed to bring "knowledge" of sin. The author of Hebrews tells us sacrificial laws serve as a "reminder of sins" (Hebrews 10:3). Paul's personal comment on sin reveals his perspective even further, "I would not have known sin except through the law" (Rom. 7:7b). Moo goes on to say,

> *The Mosaic Law, Paul claims, has brought wrath, for it has revealed sin to be transgression against God's good*

---

[188] Ibid, 338.
[189] Ibid, 338.
[190] Ibid, 338.
[191] Ibid, 324.

> *and holy law. It has thus increased Israel's responsibility (Rom. 4:15). Life under the law has led to enslavement to the "the law [or power] or sin" (Rom. 7:23), a slavery from which only Christ and his Spirit can set us free (8:2-3). "The curse of the law" stands over all who are outside of faith in Christ, for the only means of attaining righteousness apart from Christ is through perfect obedience to God's law, a feat impossible for sinful humans to accomplish (cf. Gal. 3:10, 13).[192]*

Paul continually points out this theme of humanity's futility in attempting to overcome the power of sin on one's own accord. He writes, "The Scripture declares that the whole world is a prisoner of sin" (Galatians 3:22).

Jesus and the Law

Matthew shares the best perspective concerning Jesus and His view of the Mosaic Law. In chapter 5:17-19 of Matthew's Gospel, we find an interaction where Jesus teaches His disciples and Jewish listeners about the law. Considering this interaction, Moo points out,

> *In vv. 17-19, Jesus defends himself against the charge that he is urging the abrogation of the law. Quite the contrary, Jesus claims in what is a justly famous theological summary, "I have come . . . to fulfill [the Law and the Prophets]." He then builds on this claim to continuity with the Old Testament by solemnly asserting the enduring*

---

[192] Ibid, 341.

validity of the law (v. 18) and by urging the teaching of its commandments (v. 19).[193]

"Pleroo"

There is a debate in regards to whether or not Jesus was speaking in an eschatological sense or not about using *pleroo* ("fulfill"). The thesis of this chapter holds to the view that Jesus fulfilled that which the Old Testament prophesized. Bahnsen holds to the view that Moo and this chapter are wrong in asserting such a claim. Bahnsen writes, "He has come to 'fulfill' the law by 'filling up the full measure' of its original demand (before scribal rationalizations, externalization, and qualifications: cf. vv. 21-48)."[194] Bahnsen continues to argue his perspective by pointing out a similar use of *pleroo* found in a different text, "Matthew uses it (*fulfill*) in a general sense for 'filling up' a fishnet in 13:48. It is not a word that always connotes prophecy-fulfillment."[195] An added opposing view comes from Walter Kaiser. He writes, "Even if we are unable to determine definitively what the word "fulfill" means…the subject is not about eschatological events."[196] Kaiser continues, "The antitheses of verses 17, 18, and 19 also prevent us from applying a 'prediction/verification' or a 'transcending' theme to 'fulfill.'"[197]

Conversely to Bahnsen and Kaiser, Wayne Strickland finds common ground in emphasizing his agreement with Moo. He

---

[193] Ibid, 347.
[194] Ibid, 388.
[195] Ibid, 388.
[196] Ibid, 398.
[197] Ibid, 398.

writes, "Moo has embraced a redemptive-historical approach to the Law-Gospel issue, emphasizing a baseline discontinuity between the period before and after the incarnation of Christ, a discontinuity between Mosaic Law and the Gospel of Christ. Yet he does not deny all forms of continuity, seeing 'one God, one plan, one people.'"[198] Strickland points out in regards to this particular set of verses, "His [Moo's] focus is on the Pauline contributions, recognizing the greater importance of his statements over Jesus' statements, since sometimes it is difficult to discern whether Christ's statements apply to the pre-cross situation or the post-cross situation."[199]

"Antitheses"

Jesus' six comparisons (Matthew 5:20-48), sometimes referred to as the "antitheses," further explain and clarify what the phrase "the Law and the Prophets" refers to, "the commanding aspect of the Old Testament (cf. 7:12; 22:40) rather than to the Old Testament generally. That this is the focus of v. 17 is confirmed by the shift to 'Law' in v. 18 and 'commandment' in v. 19."[200] Moo writes, "What does consistently emerge from the antitheses is Jesus' radical insistence on what he says as binding on his followers. He taught 'as one who had authority, and not as their teachers of the law' (Matthew 7:29). This independence from both Jewish tradition and from the Mosaic law itself gives us an important indicator for our interpretation of vv. 17-19."[201]

---

[198] Ibid, 401.
[199] Ibid, 403.
[200] Ibid, 350.
[201] Ibid, 350.

To be sure, any interpretation that overlooks the salvation-historical perspective of *pleroo* in v. 17 alongside the antitheses in vv. 20-48 would be, in my opinion, a mistake. It therefore seems to be that "integral to Matthew's gospel, then, is a scheme of salvation history that pictures the entire Old Testament as anticipating and pointing forward to Jesus."[202] One would be on solid theological grounds concluding Jesus "fulfills" the Mosaic Law not by exposing or prolonging it, "but by proclaiming the standards of kingdom righteousness that were anticipated in the law."[203]

Paul and the Law

As one reads the writings of Paul, it becomes apparent that Paul's teaching is in agreement with the premise discussed thus far. Paul clearly teaches that "Christians should not look directly to the Mosaic law as their authoritative code of conduct but to 'the law of Christ.' This 'law' is not a set of rules but a set of principles drawn from the life and teaching of Jesus, with love for others as its heart and the indwelling Spirit as its directive force."[204] In Romans 10:4, we find, "Christ is the end of the law [*telos nomou*], so that there may be righteousness for everyone who believes." Paul expresses, in this verse, the same concept as *pleroo* (Matthew 5:17).

---

[202] Ibid, 351.
[203] Ibid, 352.
[204] Ibid, 357.

"Nomos"

There is some debate regarding *nomos* as it is sometimes interpreted to mean legalism. However, this would not be Paul's normal use of the word. Paul, in his other writings, routinely uses *nomos* to refer specifically to the Mosaic Law.[205]

"Telos"

Additionally, the word *telos* is best understood as a culmination, fusing the concepts of both goal and end. Moo points out, "What is suggested, rather, is that the law has ceased to have a central and determinative role in God's plan and among his people."[206] Paul also points out in Galatians 5:14 and Romans 13:8-10 that love for fellow humans is the guiding principle in the new era of the "law of Christ." He further teaches "love to be so central to the law that one is not really obeying the law if love is not present."[207]

"Hypo Nomon"

Furthermore, Paul mentions "the phrase 'under [the] law' (*hypo nomon*) eleven times (Rom. 6:14, 15; 1 Cor. 9:20 [four occurrences]; Gal. 3:23; 4:4, 5, 21; 5:18)."[208] Paul strongly communicates that followers of Jesus are no longer under the Mosaic Law, meaning "under the law as a regime or power."[209] Moo rightly concludes regarding Galatians 3:15-4:7,

---

[205] Ibid, 358.
[206] Ibid, 359.
[207] Ibid, 359.
[208] Ibid, 361.
[209] Ibid, 361.

> *Paul pictures the law as something of a parenthesis within salvation history; it was "added" well after the promise to Abraham (3:17, 19) and was in effect "until the Seed to whom the promise referred had come" (3:19). It was, then, "before this faith [probably 'faith in Jesus Christ'; cf. v. 22] came" that "we were confined under the law." While we cannot be certain, it is likely that the "we" refers to Paul and other Jews. "Under the law," in fact, is only one of several phrases that Paul uses to depict the situation of the Jews in the old covenant in this context; others are "under a paidagogos" (3:25; cf. v. 24), children under "guardians and trustees" (4:1-2), "under the basic principles of the world" (4:3), and "under sin" (3:22; NIV again paraphrases).[210]*

Paul continues to assert to the Galatians that if you take one part of the law, circumcision, then you must take all parts of the law. We are not free to pick and choose what parts of the law we want. Paul's message to the believers of Galatia is to recognize the freedom we have from the law and to not put ourselves back "under the law." More importantly, as one reads the entirety of Paul's teaching, it becomes evident that he is more enthusiastic to teach followers of Jesus that they are bound to "the law of Christ."

"Ennomos Christou"

He writes, they are "not being outside the law of God but under the law of Christ" *ennomos Christou* (1 Corinthians 9:21). The literal translation means "in-lawed to Christ."[211] Moo comments, "This is perhaps the clearest Pauline statement of the situation of the Christian with respect to God's law. This 'law of

---
[210] Ibid, 361.
[211] Ibid, 368.

Christ,' the new covenant form of God's law, is not a code or series of commandments and prohibitions, but is composed of the teachings of Christ and the apostles and the directing influence of the Holy Spirit."[212]

Paul instructs us to "fulfill the law of Christ" (Galatians 6:2). We do this by referring to Paul's inspiration in (5:14), "For the entire law is fulfilled in keeping this one command: 'Love your neighbor as yourself.'" Moo summarizes, "The basic directive power of 'new covenant law' lies in the renewed heart of the Christian (Romans 12:1-2), a heart in the process of being transformed by God's Spirit into a perfect refractor and performer of God's will."[213]

The Sabbath

As a part of the Decalogue, God instituted the Sabbath for the people of Israel. Opinions on the subject, regard keeping of the Sabbath as recognition of God's creation (Exodus 31:12-17). Moreover, the people of Israel kept the Sabbath as a sign of their commitment to Yahweh's rule over them. As part of the old covenant, the requirement of keeping Sabbath was not optional. It was a part of the Mosaic Law. However, since the Sabbath, "derives not from God's nature but from his celebration of his creative work . . . Paul put the issue of keeping one day sacred in

---

[212] Ibid, 368.
[213] Ibid, 370.

the category of things that each believer could determine on the basis of his own conscience (Romans 14:5-8)."[214]

Jesus no doubt observed the Sabbath, but not the way in which the religious leaders of His day did. Jesus healed on the Sabbath and instructed the man to bring his bed home (John 5:5-8). Fascinatingly, Jesus and His disciples "violate the Sabbath by harvesting grain and 'threshing it' between their palms as they pass through a field (Luke 6:1-5)."[215] Lastly, Jesus tells the religious leaders they do not understand the real purpose of the Sabbath, "The Sabbath was made for man, not man for the Sabbath" (Mark 2:27).

Sabbatarian

Yet, the Sabbatarian viewpoint contends an "appeal to the fourth commandment and asserts that the place of the Sabbath requirement in the Decalogue meant that it is to be seen as binding moral law and normative for all people in the same way as the rest of the Decalogue (Exodus 20:11)."[216] Nevertheless, Jesus clearly taught, "his mission whether or not the Sabbath was involved" was of the most utmost importance (Luke 13:14-16, John 5:16-17). Additionally, the synoptic gospels all record Jesus as saying, "The Son of Man is Lord of the Sabbath" (Mark 2:28; cf. Matthew 12:8; Luke 6:5). Expanding on this thought, A.T. Lincoln concludes,

---

[214] Albert H. Baylis, *From Creation to the Cross* (Grand Rapids, MI: Zondervan, 1996), 127.
[215] Ibid, 134.
[216] D.A. Carson, *From Sabbath to Lord's Day* (Eugene, OR: Wipf and Stock Publishers, 1999), 354.

> *This is a momentous claim indeed when understood against the background of the Mosaic Sabbath . . . In the Old Testament, the Sabbath was said to be "a sabbath to the Lord your God" (Exod. 20:10). It belonged to Yahweh, the covenant Lord. Now here is Jesus as the Son of man claiming to be the Lord of the Sabbath. Jesus' claim to authority over the day is not only a claim to equal authority with the law given by God in which the Sabbath demand was embedded but can be understood as a claim to the same authority over the day as the covenant Lord himself, a claim to equality with God every bit as strong as the Johannine saying.*[217]

Concluding Thoughts

We clearly see from Jesus and Paul that under the new covenant, believers in Christ have the option of practicing the Sabbath, but are not bound to it as a matter of Old Testament law. Paul teaches that in Christ, "The old has gone, the new is here" (II Corinthians 5:17). The *neos* (new) applies to both the individual life of the believer regarding personal sin and sanctification and the Body of Christ's corporal link between the Mosaic Law and non-binding Gospel. Finally, Paul wrote to the Christians in Rome, "Sin is no longer your master, for you no longer live under the requirements of the law. Instead, you live under the freedom of God's grace" (Romans 6:14).

---

[217] Ibid, 363.

T.K. Anderson

CHAPTER SEVEN
Is God Alone?

A Defense of God's Self-Existence

Central to the doctrine of Christian faith is the concept of God existing *a se* from the Latin meaning "by itself." Aseity, in referring to God, is the quality of God's self-existence or complete independence of or with anything else. The theist holds, God is the greatest possible being and would exist in all possible worlds with or without anything, solely alone, and complete. As simple as this sounds, there have been many challenges and critiques over the centuries to the idea of divine aseity in referring to God. The most ardent and longstanding challenger facing the theist, finds its foundational concepts forged in the debates of ancient Greek philosophy.

Platonism is a philosophical viewpoint, which holds that alongside physical and/or concrete objects such as people, planets, and parking lots, there also exist invisible abstract objects like numbers, properties, and propositions. This poses a major problem for a theistic worldview in that if abstract objects exist *a se*, as God does, it challenges the very idea of God's uniqueness and he becomes infinitesimal and somewhat irrelevant among a myriad of other abstract objects. I will show there exists credible arguments for the theist to employ, in making sense of the quandary, between divine aseity and abstract objects.

Platonism

This ancient Greek philosophy finds its roots in none other than Plato himself. Although the point of view discussed in this chapter will lean toward a more present-day view of this philosophical ideology, the foundations extend backward in time over two thousand years. Platonism "is the view that there exist such things as abstract objects — where an abstract object is an object that does not exist in space or time and which is therefore entirely non-physical and non-mental. Platonism in this sense is a *contemporary* view. It is obviously related to the views of Plato in important ways, but it is not entirely clear that Plato endorsed this view."[218]

---

[218] Platonism in Metaphysics (revision Tue Apr 7, 2009)
http://plato.stanford.edu/entries/platonism/#5, accessed May 10, 2015

To develop this philosophy further, these abstract objects exist necessarily, meaning there would be no possible world in which these objects would not exist. J.P. Moreland writes, "It is inconceivable that there should exist, for example, a possible world lacking in numbers or propositions, even if that world were altogether devoid of concrete objects other than God himself."[219] In Platonism, the undeniable conclusion is that abstract objects exist *a se*, which brings an unsettling problem to the theist's position. There is no cause for these objects. The sheer size and scope of all possible abstract objects is mind-bending as well. Literally, there exists infinities of sets and numbers alone. In a sense, "God finds himself amid uncreated, infinite realms of beings that exist just as necessarily and independently as he."[220]

Ex Nihilo

Some theists do not accept the view of Platonism and argue against its perspective. These thinkers find the idea of God and abstract objects existing together *a se* undermining to the doctrine of creation *ex nihilo*, creation out of nothing. William Lane Craig writes, "God alone exists *a se*; all else exists *ab alio* and is therefore dependent upon God for its existence. This is a core tenet of the doctrine of God, one grounded in Scripture and tradition. If Platonism is true, then, there literally is no God."[221] Craig has a valid point in that Scripture teaches very strongly God

---

[219] J.P. Moreland & William Lane Craig, *Philosophical Foundations for a Christian Worldview* (Downers Grove, Il: InterVarsity Press, 2003), 504.
[220] Ibid, 504.
[221] William Lane Craig, "A Nominalist Perspective on God and Abstract Objects," *Philosophia Christi* 13 (2011): 305.

is the creator of all things and before Him, there was nothing. There is strong biblical support for Craig's observation and clearly, the beginning of the Gospel of John upholds the idea of God's unique status as the sole and final authority. John writes,

> *In the beginning was the Word, and the Word was with God, and the Word was God. He was in the beginning with God. All things came into being through him, and without him not one thing came into being. What has come into being in him was life, and the life was the light of all people. The light shines in the darkness, and the darkness did not overcome it.*[222]

Craig points out in his lecture on the Coherence of Theism, that John was most familiar at the time with the teaching of Greek philosophy and would have intended to include "all things" within the words that through the "Word" *Logos*, "all things came into being." Additionally, Craig points to the teachings of the early church fathers to support the view that Platonism is contrary to early church doctrine. In fact, the Nicene Creed affirms;

> *I believe in one God, the Father, Almighty, Maker of heaven and earth and of all things visible and invisible;*
>
> *And in one Lord, Jesus Christ, the only Son of God, begotten of the Father before all ages, light from light, true God from true God, begotten not made, consubstantial with the Father, through whom all things came into being.*

---

[222] The Holy Bible, *Gospel of John Chapter 1:1-5* (New Revised Standard Version, 1989)

Craig explains, "The phrase "Maker of heaven and earth and of all things visible and invisible" derives from Paul, and the expression "through whom all things came into being" from the prologue to John's Gospel. The Council affirms that everything other than God was created by God through the Son, so that God alone is uncreated."[223]

Nominalism

Craig finds a rejoinder to Platonism and abstract objects in the concept of Nominalism. The biblical data and early church doctrine motivate Craig to search for a solution. Although he is not absolutely settled on this perspective, he finds it a best alternative for a theist. Craig finds a type of, or modification of his own, in this view, on account of nominalist perspectives having various meanings in philosophical discussions today. Craig writes in the Oxford Studies in Philosophy of Religion,

> *...if a Christian theist is to be a Platonist, then, he must, it seems, embrace Absolute Creationism, the view that God has created all the abstract objects there are. Those of us who find the boot-strapping problem compelling, however, must look elsewhere to find some solution to the problem posed by the existence of uncreatables. In recent decades there has been a proliferation of nominalistic treatments of abstract objects which has served to make Nominalism an attractive alternative for the orthodox theist. Van Inwagen himself holds that there is rightly a strong*

---

[223] William Lane Craig, Coherence of Theism Conference (Marietta, GA: Biola University, April 17-18, 2015)

presumption of Nominalism's truth which only a rationally compelling argument for Platonism can overcome. Even if we do not hold to such a presumption, the orthodox Christian who is not an Absolute Creationist has grounds for thinking that Platonism is false and therefore has powerful reasons for entertaining Nominalism. Unless all forms of Nominalism can be shown to be untenable, the orthodox Christian can on theological grounds rationally embrace Nominalism as a viable alternative to Platonism.[224]

Not Always An Easy Fix

Paul Gould disagrees with Craig's perspective on this issue. Gould in an extensive article in Philosophia Christi remarks, "The open question then is this: Is Nominalism explanatorily superior (not merely equal) to realist accounts of various phenomena? It is not clear that it is and thus it is not clear that Nominalism represents the best option for the traditional theist, and certainly not the only option."[225] The fact that Nominalism holds there are no abstract objects, only particulars, seems like an easy fix and solution to the difficulty presented by Platonism. Nonetheless, Gould reasons that a presumption of Nominalism, as argued by Peter van Inwagen, is not a clear option. Gould accepts a "traditional theist can be a Nominalist"[226] but questions "whether she should be."[227] His basis for apprehension is a concern for what

---

[224] William Lane Craig, Oxford Studies in Philosophy of Religion Volume 4 (Oxford Scholarship Online: January 2013) http://www.oxfordscholarship.com/view/10.1093/acprof:oso/9780199656417.001.0001/acprof-9780199656417-chapter-3, accessed May 5, 2015.
[225] Paul Gould, Philosophia Christi Vol. 13 No. 2 2011, 274. http://www.paul-gould.com/wp-content/uploads/2012/03/art-Gould1.pdf, accessed May 1, 2015.
[226] Ibid, 271.
[227] Ibid, 271.

is the "best theory of the mind-language-world nexus." Gould does not think Nominalism provides the best theory.

Alongside Gould, R. Scott Smith has difficulties in accepting Craig's solution to the Platonist – Abstract Object (P-AO) dilemma. Smith writes,

> *Instead of Platonism, Craig sees much promise for a nominalist view of properties.* [228] *He disavows the nominalist options (such as trope theory) that would affirm their existence, yet cash them out as particulars. Instead, he takes the route of denying the existence of properties. Besides God and created, contingent AOs, on his view, only concrete particulars that are located in space and time really exist.* [229]

It is important to note that on Craig's view, there are "qualitative facts that exist"[230] as Smith writes. For example, grass really is green, and I am thinking of giving my dog a snack. Additionally, it is interesting to note that even though it may be a popular choice to embrace Physicalism alongside the nominalist perspective, Craig does not do so. Craig holds that immaterial essences in the form of qualitative facts do exist and are "immaterial…and spatially and temporally located."[231] Ultimately, Craig seems to rely on Carnac's view of meanings and linguistic

---

[228] While he remains open to conceptualism, Craig seems intent on pursuing nominalism: "While conceptualism remains a fallback position should all forms of nominalism fail, I think that the alternatives afforded by nominalism are far from exhausted and merit exploration" ("Anti-Platonism," 115).
[229] R. Scott Smith, *Craig's Nominalism and the High Cost of Preserving Divine Aseity* (Biola University, CSSR 660 MD1 SpTpcs: Coherence of Theism course 2014), 3.
[230] Ibid, 3.
[231] Ibid, 3.

framework. R. Scott Smith rebuts this view of Nominalism from Craig in showing that if we do away with essences and true meaning, then we do away with the truth of Scripture and even some of Craig's philosophical perspectives as well, such as his Kalam Cosmological argument.

Furthermore, it becomes a strange circle to utilize words to describe a philosophical view that describes a perspective that words or language have no true meaning. There is much more to expand on this topic, however the scope of the chapter will limit my comments and discovery. But for now, it is safe to conclude that Craig feels as though he's found a coherent balance on the issue with an anti-realism perspective. Gould and Smith feel as though there is not.

Divine Conceptualism

For the vast majority of Christian history, theologians have held to a view of Divine Conceptualism. Augustine adopted this view and his writings have been instrumental in proliferating this view for centuries. To Augustine, abstract objects somehow existed in the mind of God. It would be agreeable, under this view, to consider AO's as divine ideas. As such, ideas are conceptualized and hold reality but in the mind of God, not independent of Him, and not outside of His mind. The Platonic forms of propositions and properties all exist but are all ideas directed by and coming from the mind of God. As such, the proposition of 4+4=8 and the property of greenness really do exist but as concepts in God's domain. Gould brings a bit more clarity to the discussion by explaining that "abstract objects are identified with various constituent entities of the divine mind and are uncreated yet dependent upon God. Just how the dependency relation is to be understood is an open question."[232] It is important to note, with this view, that divine substance is the ultimate origin and thus AO's are (at some level) causally dependent and ultimately contingent upon God.

In God's Mind

Conceptualism is attractive as it offers a conceivable solution to the P-AO predicament. Being that God's ideas belong squarely in God's mind, AO's would not be a part of the created order. AO's are eternal and uncreated because God is eternal and uncreated. Just as God's moral intuition and character is a part of His nature, so numbers and logic are imbedded in God's mind. J.P. Moreland comments, "Just as moral values are rooted in the moral nature of God such that his moral commands are necessary expression of his nature, so the divine mind operates in accord with logically necessary truths. The necessity of logic and mathematics may be seen as grounded in the necessity of God's intellect."[233] Additionally, if AO's are conceived in the mind of God, they do not "exist explanatorily prior to God's conception of them."[234] Gould goes on to explain, "Thus, realism holds at the

---

[232] Paul Gould, *Philosophia Christi* Vol. 13 No. 2 2011, 269. http://www.paul-gould.com/wp-content/uploads/ 2012/03/art-Gould1.pdf, accessed May 1, 2015.
[233] J.P. Moreland & William Lane Craig, *Philosophical Foundations for a Christian Worldview* (Downers Grove, Il: InterVarsity Press, 2003), 506.
[234] Ibid, 506.

human level and conceptualism at the divine level. That is, relative to finite minds, abstract objects exist as realistically as any Platonic entity… But abstract objects do not exist realistically for God, in the sense that they exist apart from or over and above God. Rather, their existence is purely conceptual."[235]

Two Problems

Modified Platonists have two main problems with Divine Conceptualism. First, it blurs a thought with its thing. Consider someone who is thinking about the color green as it is embodied in a patch of grass on your front lawn. The actual green of the grass resides in the mind of the individual only as it relates to the person focusing on the patch of grass. If you contrast that to a person who is thinking about greenness, the very thought of being green becomes a "constituent" of the person's mind. J.P. Moreland explains,

> *Thus a concept in the mind is not identical to the object of the mind that has the concept. God's various concepts of abstract objects are within his mind, but the objects of those concepts – various abstract objects themselves – are not. On this point, the critic sides with those that believe that universals are instantiated by their possessors, God included, against the conceptualist notion that the universal is abstracted from the particular.*[236]

Conceptualists respond to this by noting the difference between the greenness that exists in the grass and the universal

---
[235] Paul Gould, Philosophia Christi Vol. 13 No. 2 2011, 270. http://www.paul-gould.com/wp-content/uploads/ 2012/03/art-Gould1.pdf, accessed May 1, 2015.
[236] J.P. Moreland & William Lane Craig, *Philosophical Foundations for a Christian Worldview* (Downers Grove, Il: InterVarsity Press, 2003), 506.

property of greenness that is a conceptual entity. They describe greenness as the divine concept that exists as a mind-independent reality, which exists in the grass as an abstract particular.[237] Moreland goes on to explain the conceptualists response, "Such concepts may or may not have mind-independent correlates, as is evident in cases in which one thinks of creatures of fiction or logically impossible entities like a square circle. Abstract objects are God's concepts, and if he has concepts of abstract objects, then those are concepts of his concepts."[238]

A second liability charged to the conceptualist's viewpoint is similar to an objection the modified Platonist faces as well. Essentially, if God is the creator of all properties, then He must be prior to those properties being created. This becomes a challenge because God would have to have those properties to create the very properties He desires to create. Again Moreland comments, "For the divine mind is not identical to its concepts; the divine mind has or contains them…God and his mind must exist causally and explanatorily prior to his concepts. Thus conceptualism seems to face the same problem raised against modified Platonism."[239]

Conceptualists respond in agreement that, the "universal properties that God exemplifies are concepts in God's mind."[240] However, that does not preclude the idea that prior to God

---

[237] Correlated from J.P. Moreland & William Lane Craig, *Philosophical Foundations for a Christian Worldview* (Downers Grove, Il: InterVarsity Press, 2003), 507.
[238] Ibid, 507.
[239] Ibid, 506.
[240] Ibid, 507.

conceptualizing omniscience, He cannot be, by His very nature, all-knowing.

Modified Platonism

Of most recent, historically speaking, some Christian philosophers have advanced a view that abstract objects can exist necessarily, but do not necessarily exist *a se*. They posit that the balance between the competing correlates can be achieved. It is a view that AO's can exist in every possible world and are just as much created beings, as are physical objects. This view maintains, "They are not created by God at any *time* but rather are *timelessly* created by him. God is not temporally prior to the existence of such objects, but he is causally or explanatorily prior to their existence."[241] Two problems seem to block this modest resolution.

Is God Free to Create?

The first problem points out that because AO's exist necessarily, they would exist outside of and free of God's will. This is a major issue for the Modified Platonist perspective since it becomes a direct challenge to God's sovereignty and control of all creation. God loses all freedom from refusing to create such entities. This becomes an issue due to a principal doctrine fundamental to the Christian faith that God is free to create at will and all of creation is of His free will. Clarified by Moreland as,

---

[241] Ibid, 504.

"had he wished, (God) could have remained alone without any exigency of producing a world of creatures."[242]

How does the modified Platonist view respond to this challenge? God is completely unrestricted from creating contingent beings, however He is not able to "refrain from sustaining abstract objects in existence."[243] At first blush, this seems to be a real problem, however when looking deeper, it amounts to nothing more than God not being able to refrain from making green the number two or other such notions. Is it really a problem that God cannot make 1+1=5 or that yellow is not a taste? J.P. Moreland continues, "Virtually all Christian theists have held that mathematical and logical truths do not lie within the scope of God's will, and the same is true for the nature of and relations among various abstract objects. It may be said that all these 'limitations' on God's freedom are actually pseudotasks and thus not real limitations."[244]

The Bootstrap Objection

The second, more serious problem for Modified Platonism is the bootstrapping objection. This is similar to the same objection faced by Divine Conceptualism. The basic problem is best explained by Gould, "God has properties. If God is the creator of all things, then God is the creator of his properties. But God can't create properties unless he already has the property of being able to create a property. Thus, we are off to the races, ensnared in

---
[242] Ibid, 505.
[243] Ibid, 505.
[244] Ibid, 505.

a vicious explanatory circle."[245] Craig additionally utilizes the bootstrapping objection against Platonism. Nonetheless Smith, Moreland, and Gould maintain there is a coherent reply to this quandary. Smith writes,

> Now Craig rightly objects to Morris and Menzel's Absolute Creationism, for God would have to create His own properties, a view that not only is incoherent, but also unbiblical. But why should theists who also are Platonists embrace their view? Why couldn't they embrace approaches such as advocated by Gould or Moreland? For example Gould suggests the obvious solution to Morris and Menzel's view is to maintain that "all of God's essential properties (that is, divine concepts) exist a se as a brute fact within the divine mind, and it is only those properties that are not essentially exemplified by God (that is, necessarily satisfied in God) that are created by God.[246]

Critics may counter this response as being ad hoc and not adequate. The Modified Platonist would be free to respond that there is no conflict to the idea of God being loving, being forgiving, and being great; and being powerful is in any way incoherent. These properties of God are simply who He is and these properties exist necessarily as a brute fact. Therefore, love and other abstract qualities or objects can and do exist timeless and created by God either on account of His nature or because of His nature. Therefore, I find this view to be the most coherent in

---

[245] Paul Gould, "The Problem of God and Abstract Objects: A Prolegomenon," *Philosophia Christi* 13 (2011): 259.
[246] R. Scott Smith, "William Lane Craig's Nominalism, Essences, and Implications for Our knowledge of Reality," *Philosophia Christi* Vol. 15, No. 2 (2013): 153.

regards to theology, philosophy, and in uniformity with biblical accounts of God and His properties. J.P. Moreland concludes, "The Modified Platonist solution provides a way to reconcile these two justified beliefs, and that is a virtue of the approach."[247]

Conclusion

Having discussed and surveyed three possible resolutions to the problem of divine aseity and abstract objects, we have seen that the theist stands firm on a solid foundation in defending the aseity of God. Nominalism, Divine Conceptualism, and Modified Platonism all provide a distinctive perspective within a coherent framework to God's existence *a se*. Remarkably, the theist can find assurance in the Platonist or Anti-Platonist position.

The dialogue really turns on which of these philosophical perspectives best match the biblical description of God's nature and theological implications of its respective position? As a concluding note to this dialog, I would tend to agree with Gould in saying, "There is no simple solution to the problem of God and abstract objects."[248] Nevertheless, "it is reasonable to think that just as all of reality somehow points to the divine, so too all knowledge. And surely God has created us to know him and his created world, which includes abstract objects. So, there is reason to hope, following Anselm, that by faith we can come to understand the reality in question as well."[249]

---

[247] J.P. Moreland & William Lane Craig, *Philosophical Foundations for a Christian Worldview* (Downers Grove, Il: InterVarsity Press, 2003), 505.
[248] Paul Gould, "The Problem of God and Abstract Objects: A Prolegomenon," *Philosophia Christi* 13 (2011): 274.
[249] Ibid, 274.

CHAPTER EIGHT
What About The Crusades?

The Modern View

Cursory appraisals of the Crusades as depicted by modern-day politicians, historians, media outlets, and pop culture describe the events in a context unbecoming to the Christian faith. In many cases, the Crusades are used to justify the atrocities of the more recent Islamic extremist movement. If not done so in an act to rationalize, at a minimum, it is done to mitigate judgment as to appear tolerant toward all cultures. In 2001, after Muslim jihadists attacked the United States, former President Bill Clinton stated in a speech at Georgetown University, "When the Christian soldiers took Jerusalem [1099], they…proceeded to kill every woman and child who was Muslim on the Temple Mount." Mr. Clinton continued by saying this story was "still being told today in the

Middle East and we are still paying for it."[250] More recently, in response to the brutal Charlie Hebdo attack in Paris, President Barak Obama in his speech at the National Prayer Breakfast remarked, "And lest we get on our high horse and think this is unique to some other place, remember that during the Crusades and the Inquisition, people committed terrible deeds in the name of Christ. In our home country, slavery and Jim Crow all too often was justified in the name of Christ."[251]

This type of narrow commentary is common among academia and in the entertainment field as well. One reliable Western history book comments, "the Crusades fused three characteristic medieval impulses piety, pugnacity, and greed. All three were essential."[252] The popular film starring Orlando Bloom, *Kingdom of Heaven* (2005), depicts European crusaders destroying and ransacking Muslim communities consumed with a voracious thirst for more. The pop culture scene of role-playing games weigh in on the topic with historical statements such as "The soldiers of the First Crusade appeared basically without warning, storming into the Holy Land with the avowed literally task of slaughtering unbelievers";[253] "The Crusades were an early sort of imperialism;"[254] and "Confrontation with Islam gave birth to a period of religious fanaticism that spawned the terrible Inquisition

---

[250] Paul Crawford, *Four Myths about the Crusades*, accessed December 3, 2015, http://www.catholicnewsagency.com/column/four-myths-about-the-crusades-1562/
[251] Anthony Zurcher, *Obama's 'high horse': IS, the Crusades and moral equivalency*, accessed December 1, 2015, http://www.bbc.com/news/blogs-echochambers-31156153
[252] Warren Hollister, J. Sears McGee, and Gale Stokes, The West Transformed: A History of Western
Civilization, vol. 1 (New York: Cengage/Wadsworth, 2000), 311.
[253] R. Scott Peoples, Crusade of Kings (Rockville, MD: Wildside, 2009), 7.
[254] Ibid.

and the religious wars that ravaged Europe during the Elizabethan era."[255] Historian Sir Steven Runciman concluded a three-volume work by writing the crusades were "nothing more than a long act of intolerance in the name of God, which is the sin against the Holy Ghost."[256]

The Historical View

According to the above statements, the case is settled. A verdict has been rendered and the crusades were nothing more than bloodthirsty European nobility, with the backing and influence of the malicious Roman Catholic Church, invading a peaceful and tolerant Muslim world. The relentless Christian attacks, in an overt attempt to convert the devout and peace-loving world of Islam, was an egregious act of violence perpetrated upon the innocent. The question remains however, is this historical narrative accurate? Not according to author Rodney Stark, he writes, "the Crusades were precipitated by Islamic provocations: by centuries of bloody attempts to colonize the West and by sudden new attacks on Christian pilgrims and holy places. Although the Crusades were initiated by a plea from the Pope, this had nothing to do with the hopes of converting Islam."[257] The crusades are a complex tapestry of diverse motivations yet can be defensible through a proper view of history and a well-structured

---
[255] The Crusades: Campaign Sourcebook, ed. Allen Varney (Lake Geneva, WI: TSR, 1994), 2.
[256] Sir Steven Runciman, A History of the Crusades: Vol. III, The Kingdom of Acre and the Later Crusades
(Cambridge: Cambridge University Press, 1954), 480.
[257] Rodney Stark, God's Battalions (New York, NY: HarperOne, 2009), 8.

response. Therefore, it would be inadequate and prejudicial to assess a topic as broad and deep as the crusades in a hurried manner.

Nine Hundred Years

The crusades, as most notably discussed, usually refer to a two-hundred-year period ranging from 1095–1290 AD. During this time period, there indeed was a fierce battle within the territories stretching from Constantinople, through Jerusalem, and to Cairo. Most certainly, the battle was between European armies, with full support from the Church, and the armies of the Muslim world. However, the most striking feature regarding this topic is the historical connecting points literally stretching from the mid-seventh century for almost nine hundred years into the sixteenth century. The crusading movement has its deep roots embedded within the effects of the early stages of the Islamic expansion and stretched far into the territories of Spain, Scandinavia, and Baltic lands well into the sixteenth century.

The crusades then, are literally a nine-hundred-year analysis stretching over three continents, multiple kingdoms, a variety of languages, and diverse religious views. To simplify the entirety of this historical tapestry, spanning nine centuries and multiple lands, to the perspective of Church-sponsored Christian soldiers invading and subsequently occupying the Levant for a two hundred year duration is to be facetious in the approach.

Taking a step backwards however, it would be difficult to survey the entirety of this historical scope within such a restricted response. For sake of argument, the limitations of this response will eliminate the crusading movement past the thirteen-century but will not be self-limiting to the eminent call to take the cross. There is no doubt to some that "the crusading movement began in 1095 when Pope Urban II (1088-99) proclaimed to a sort of revival meeting in Clermont, France, that "God wills" the rescue of the Holy Land from Islam."[258] Pope Urban II's appeal to free the Holy Land was occasioned by a call for help from the Byzantine Empire. The Orthodox Church in Constantinople was experiencing an incontestable onslaught from Turkish warlords. Within this context,

> *A just cause was in the mind of Pope Urban II when he preached the First Crusade, a move he may have been considering for some years. In the first week of March 1095 a council of bishops from France, Italy and Germany was in session at Piacenze. To it came an embassy from the Byzantine emperor Alexius I Comnenus, appealing to the Pope to encourage Westerners to help defend the Eastern Church against the Turks, who had swept through Asia Minor and had almost reached Constantinople.[259]*

To gain a full viewpoint of the call for help, issued from the Byzantine Empire, we must go back in time four hundred years to gain the perspective and urgency embroidered within this

---

[258] Mark A. Noll, Turning Points Third Edition (Grand Rapids, MI: Baker Academic, 2012), 130.
[259] Jonathan Riley-Smith, What Were the Crusades? (San Francisco, CA: Ignatius Press, 2009), 12.

request. In the early seventh century, through the prophet Muhammad in Mecca, the Islamic religion began. Over the succeeding generations, the Muslim faith rapidly spread over the Near East, not by conversion of the heart but through a subjugation of the will buttressed with the threat of death and military conquest. This was truly a "Muslim invasion of Christendom."[260]

How Christianity Grew

On the contrary, from the time of the mid to late first century, Christianity spread from its founding in Jerusalem throughout the entire Mediterranean world through conversions of the heart and a freedom of the will. It is well attested that through the message and lives of the apostles, and leadership of the early church, the Christian centers of influence were established in the ancient cities of Constantinople, Antioch, Alexandria, Jerusalem, and Rome. Additionally, Nicaea held a distinctive space in the heart of the Christian world as the foundation of the Nicene Creed in 325 AD.

With the conversion of Constantine in the early fourth century, Christianity became the official religion of the Roman Empire, thereby stretching from Spain throughout the Near East. It is of particular interest to note that Christianity never attempted forced conversions or military takeover of other lands prior to the late eleventh century. Throughout the early formation of the church, leaders encouraged a pacifist approach to conflict. Once

---

[260] Rodney Stark, God's Battalions (New York, NY: HarperOne, 2009), 9.

the Roman state merged with the authority of the Church, Augustine and other church leaders championed a just war theory that detailed specific guidelines in which war could be a proper course of action. It mostly centered on a defensive option in combination with a lawful declaration by those in authority.

How Islam Grew

At the time of the spread of Islam, in the seventh and eighth centuries, the great centers of Christianity had been firmly established for hundreds of years. However, with the fall of the Roman Empire, some of those Near East and North African centers of faith were weakened militarily. It was in this context that Muslim invaders conquered the former Christian cities and subjugated any remaining followers of Christ to a combination of slavery or lower economic status and all under Islamic rule and law. They destroyed numerous Christian churches, libraries, and structures. The Muslim conquest of the Near East and Northern Africa did not stop there. In the ensuing periods of the ninth, tenth, and eleventh centuries, Muslim conquers continued to occupy and attack Spain, France, Italy, Turkey, and attempted to gain control of most island nations throughout the Mediterranean Sea.

When the Constantinopolitan appeal for help arrived in Pope Urban II's court, Robert the Monk has the pope proclaim,

> *They [the Turks] have completely destroyed some of God's churches and they have converted others to the uses of their own cult. They ruin the altars with filth and defilement. They circumcise Christians and smear the*

> blood from the circumcision over the altars or throw it into the baptismal fonts. They are pleased to kill other by cutting open their bellies, extracting the end of their intestines, and tying it to a stake. Then, with flogging, they drive their victims around the stake until, when their viscera have spilled out, they fall dead on the ground. They tie others, again, to stakes and shoot arrows at them; they seize others, stretch out their necks, and try to see whether they can cut off their heads with a single blow of a naked sword. And what shall I say about the shocking rape of women?[261]

There is no doubt this charged language was used to elicit a response from the nobles of France and Germany. Nonetheless, the historical accuracy of the claims was not in question. France had beaten back brutal assaults on its native soil. The Italian coastal cities had been relentlessly attacked for generations. Spain was in the midst of a near four hundred year conflict with the Moors. The once great Christian cities of Jerusalem, Antioch, Alexandria, and Nicaea were under Muslim rule, and now Constantinople was in risk of being overrun. Medieval historian Paul Crawford, Ph.D. writes, "Two-thirds of the formerly Roman Christian world was now ruled by Muslims."[262] It is fair to conclude that Pope Urban II's call to crusade was not a call to occupy a peaceful land, or a desire to convert an entire religious group, nor motivated by selfish gain found within the spoils or war. The call to take the cross was motivated in part to defend Christendom and restore that which had been so brutally taken.

---

[261] From the account of Robert the Monk, *Historia Hierosolimitana,* in James A. Brundage, The Crusades: A Documentary Survey (Milwaukee, WI: Marquette University Press, 1962), 18.
[262] Paul Crawford, *Four Myths about the Crusades*, accessed December 4, 2015, http://www.catholicnewsagency.com/column/four-myths-about-the-crusades-1562/

"Just War" Taken Too Far

It would be unfair at this point to end the discussion within a Christian context justifying the crusading events following the Byzantine emperor's invitation; for what followed in terms of conduct of the Christian world was anything but in agreement with the teachings of Christ as found in the Gospels. Just War Theory as developed by Augustine was used as a support to unite the kings, nobles, and peasants of Western Europe. The ideology of rightly defending one's homeland was however extracted beyond its intended structure.

As the First Crusade ensued, the armies marched to Constantinople and accomplished their goal of bolstering the defenses of this great Christian city. From there, the armies of the First Crusade marched across Turkey and eventually to Jerusalem and accomplished the mission of regaining the Holy Land, in the name of Christ. The perfidious behavior of mass murders, destruction, and callous treatment of women and children bore an ugly resemblance of bitterness and hatred for Jewish and Muslim people. These were not the marks of one rightly defending the onslaught of marauding forces. The subsequent crusades and longstanding occupation were littered with bloody conflicts and less than Christian ideals.

This is a hard challenge to answer. One can define the underlying motivation and desire for the crusading movement; however, the way in which it was carried out seems to be in contradiction with the very nature of Jesus' teachings. So, a second question now remains, what is a reasoned apologetic response to the crusading events knowing it is near impossible to offer a satisfactory defense of the behavior regarding those who conducted its mission?

A Response

No Excuse

First, there is no excuse for random killing, blatant destruction, rampant militarism, and callous treatment of prisoners, non-combatants, women, or children. There are no biblical grounds for much of the behavior regarding the unbridled and pent-up anger of a majority of the crusading forces. One must keep in mind however, the discipline and structure of our modern military warfare was not present a thousand years ago within the ranks of local noblemen and their individual forces. It is true they were on a mission from the Church to redeem the Holy Land. It is true they took up the cross in an attempt to defend what they felt was taken. It is true that they carried the name of Christ into battle. However, it is also true they were mistaken in many of their actions.

A Medieval Structure

However, an additional point to study is the connection to and reliance upon the structure of the Church within the European kingdoms. Unlike our modern culture where a clear line of division exists between Church and State, in the Medieval world, it was more like a patch quilt of nation states wherein the Church functioned as a thread to tie it all together. In today's world, when America goes to battle, it is not considered a Christian war, even though "eighty-three percent of Americans identify themselves as Christians."[263] The religious faith of a nation is not attached to the actions of its military involvement. As a society, we have developed a clear distinction between being and acting as a citizen in comparison to a particular system of faith—not so in centuries past. To be a part of a particular nation was to be the faith of that nation.

The authority and influence of the Church implanted by Constantine seven hundred years prior, in part drove this. The authority and dependence upon the Church and its leadership in matters of faith and war was widely accepted within all classes of society. The connection between the two great institutions was almost inseparable. The Church, in a sense, bore the responsibility along with the State to protect the people and therefore the lands. That sense of responsibility drove the Church leaders to partner with and endorse military powers in the name of Christ to defend the lands and therefore their flock. No such responsibility for Christian leaders exists in today's world.

Abandoning the Foundation

A third point to contemplate rests in the notion that individuals and groups can stray from their original foundations.

---

[263] Gary Langer, *Poll: Most Americans Say They're Christian*, Accessed December 8, 2015, http://abcnews.go.com/US/story?id=90356&page=1

As such, it does not therefore follow that the foundational truths of those individuals or group is in truth faulty. One charge levied against the truth of the Christian faith is the behavior found within the decisions of the popes and church leaders of this medieval time period. It is fair to say many of the decisions and theological reasoning drawn upon by the Christian leaders of that day is not in agreement with almost all Christian leaders of today. This of course is no surprise, since it would be likewise difficult to find any agreement between this medieval world and the original apostles or early Church fathers. Simply put, the errors of those generations do not negate the truth claims of Christianity anymore than do the scientific errors of past scientists negate the findings of today's discoveries. It is possible for a culture, religiously based, to lose its foundation and drift into unintended consequences unfamiliar to the foundational truths of the original premise. The disappointment of the crusading era is only emancipated by the self-correction of the subsequent period of the Reformation.

Penance-Based

A fourth element to ponder understands the fighting element in combination with the spiritual makeup of the people in the dark ages. It was largely a penance-based society where one must earn salvation through a set of good works. Stark writes,

> *"Pilgrimage can be defined as 'a journey undertaken from religious motives to a sacred place.' Among Christians, especially in the West, the 'religious motives' increasingly had to do with atonement – with obtaining forgiveness for*

one's sins. Some who made the long journey were seeking forgiveness for the accumulated sins of a lifetime."[264]

With the possibility of future pilgrimages being unavailable, the core of one's salvation was at risk. This mindset not only permeated the lower and working class of the time period, but even more was this deep spiritual need to receive forgiveness also a driving force with the nobility. In fact, Pope Urban II's call to crusade was in part driven by this very connection between seeking spiritual forgiveness and a natural bent toward battle.

That even very pious knights found pacifism incomprehensible may puzzle some having modern sensibilities, but that assumption was fundamental to Pope Urban's call for a Crusade. Having come from a family of noble knights, the pope took their propensity for violence for granted. He fully understood that from early childhood a knight was raised to regard fighting as his chief function and that throughout 'his life the knight spent most of this time in practicing with his arms or actually fighting. Since the pope could not get the knights of Europe to observe a peace of God, at least he could enlist them to serve in God's battalions and to direct their fierce bravery toward a sacred cause. And to bring this about, Urban proposed something entirely new – that participation in the Crusade was the moral equivalent of serving in a monastic order, in that special holiness and certainty of salvation would be gained by those who took part.[265]

---

[264] Rodney Stark, God's Battalions (New York, NY: HarperOne, 2009), 87.
[265] Ibid, 106.

Finding The Way Back

Fortunately, even though the process was lengthy, the Church freed itself from this contradictory thinking. By the sixteenth century, through the work of reformers like Wycliffe, Huss, Luther, and Calvin, Christianity found its way back to the truth of its foundation as found in Romans 1:17, "For in it the righteousness of God is revealed from faith for faith, as it is written, 'The righteous shall live by faith'."

Equal Justice

Lastly, a final point to consider rests in the concept of equal justice. There are some who hold Christians of the crusading period in harsh judgment, yet seemingly withhold judgment from Muslim counterparts. What seems to be missing is that equality in judgment demands equal judgment. If one wishes to harshly judge the Christians of that era, equal justice demands the same toward the Muslims of that period. It then follows; the same level of judgment applies to today, to the recent actions of any militant 'crusading' extremist groups, regardless of the religious affiliation – Christian or Muslim. This concept can and should be pushed a step further. It is easy to evaluate the behavior and actions of others through the lens of history. We can clearly see from our vantage point the errors and inconsistency of past actions. However, what equal justice demands is for our current actions to be judged on the same playing field. It is tempting to look at the faults and failures of others, yet miss the very inadequacies within one's own life. Lest we be guilty of hypocrisy, one should be very careful to issue judgments upon the actions of others without first coming to terms with our own personal failings.

Concluding Thoughts

In summary, the crusading era was in response to a centuries-long provocation from Muslim invaders. Although the early church or today's current leaders would not have supported this type of Christian response, it was an expected response fitting within the religious and societal norms of that day. The desire to redeem the Holy Land, protect pilgrimages, and secure Christendom was most certainly the motivation. Yet many of the actions were not in keeping with the teachings of Christ. A coherent reaction to the Crusades keeps in mind the spiritual approach of the day, the unique connection between the Church and nobility, recalling that entire nations and groups can lose their way, while remembering equal justice requires looking in prior to looking out. By the grace of God, the Church found its way back to the foundational truths of Christ and the period of crusading faded into the past.

T.K. Anderson

CHAPTER NINE
Is Disbelief in God Reasonable?
& The Parable of The Dancing Monkeys

> *An Illusion: But Who's*

Great magicians of the world have one undeniable characteristic in common, the capacity to craft amazing illusions of grandeur. Through cunning deception, strikingly beautiful choreography, and years of unrelenting training, these purveyors of illusionary wonder skillfully entertain us, even in a skeptically rational society. Within this agreed-upon deception, however, rests a powerful truth; that is, humans are woefully susceptible to self-deception in exchange for a type of emotional or intellectual psychological trade-off. The good news is, in many situations throughout life, this sort of self-deception is harmless and in some cases beneficial. In sudden cases of death, tragedy, or overwhelming circumstances, our auto-coping mechanism is adeptly prepared to bring us through some pretty tough times.

Nonetheless, from a psychological standpoint, we call this type of behavior cognitive dissonance. An example of this kind of behavior would be an employee who was passed over for a promotion. Instead of an honest self-evaluation regarding one's recent job performance, lifetime experience, or educational qualifications, the employee concludes the boss must be guilty of discrimination, nepotism, or simply does not like him. The employee goes on to conclude he did not want the promotion because he has more freedom in his current position. We use "these rationalizations to reduce the psychological discomfort of holding contradictory beliefs or thoughts ('cognitions')."[266] The employee wants to believe he is qualified for the job and that no one else is more qualified than he is. Furthermore, he does not want to admit to the fact that he did not receive a promotion due to his lack of merit alone. It is psychologically easier to ignore the facts.

A similar type of cognitive dissonance often takes place when the discussion turns away from magicians or employment and centers upon one's belief in God and the validity of Biblical Christianity. For instance, humanity has collected more facts and figures regarding a Divine source for our existence than at any other time in history, yet some still hold that God does not exist and that Christianity is a fairy tale. I suggest it is possible and likely probable that those who hold to this belief are suffering from self-deception. Mitch Stokes writes,

---

[266] Neel Burton, MD, "Self-Deception I: Rationalization." *Psychology Today,* March 10, 2012, accessed December 1, 2016, https://www.psychologytoday.com/blog/hide-and-seek/201203/self-deception-i-rationalization

> *I understand why some people are skeptical about religion. What I don't understand is how naïve some atheists are about the rational strength of their position. It's one thing to believe there's no God, but it's quite another to say things like, "there exists not a shred of respectable evidence" for God's existence, or "science shows that God does not exist."[267] When atheists make such grand claims, they're either frightfully ignorant of the relevant complexities or else bluffing. In either case, they should stop, if for no other reason than that they're damaging their credibility.[268]*

Stokes hits the nail on the head with his assessment of the modern-day new-atheists. I will argue in this chapter that those who elect not to believe the substantial philosophical evidence pointing to a Creator do so for reasons not connected to a requisite amount of evidence deemed necessary for one to make a conclusion that belief in God is logical.

Keeping An Open Mind

To be fair, not all atheists or agnostics hold to the boisterous views of Hitchens, Stenger, Dawkins, Krauss, or Harris. Some individuals have yet to hear or read of a compelling case for belief in God and are holding their personal decision in abeyance, awaiting more study and personal research. Others battle with issues of doubt, false information, or personal disappointments but

---

[267] The first is from Christopher Hitchens' introduction to Christopher Hitchens, ed., *The Portable Atheist: Essential Readings for the Nonbeliever* (Philadelphia: Da Capo, 2007), xxii; the second is from the subtitle to Victor J. Stenger, *God: The Failed Hypothesis–How Science Shows That God Does Not Exist* (Amherst, NY: Prometheus, 2008), cited in Mitch Stokes, *How to be an atheist: Why Skeptics Aren't Skeptical Enough* (Wheaton, Il: Crossway, 2016), 13.

[268] Mitch Stokes, *How to be an atheist: Why Skeptics Aren't Skeptical Enough* (Wheaton, Il: Crossway, 2016), 13.

are open to learning more. To that end, I invite you to journey through this introspective writing, exploring compelling philosophical reasons for God's existence and lighting the path toward Biblical Christianity. To fulfill the mandate of the thesis, it is incumbent upon the author to provide the reader with a sufficient amount of rational contemplation that point to the soundness of the claim.

Aesop's Fable

I will begin by addressing four major philosophical arguments to support the *case* for God. Before moving on to some of the more heavy material, I would like to introduce a pertinent tale entitled *The Dancing Monkeys*. This not-so-famous Aesop fable suggests that not everything one sees is what it appears to be. The story is told,

> *A Prince had some monkeys trained to dance. Being naturally great mimics of men's actions, they showed themselves most apt pupils, and when arrayed in their rich clothes and masks, they danced as well as any of the courtiers. The spectacle was often repeated with great applause, till on one occasion a courtier, bent on mischief, took from his pocket a handful of nuts and threw them upon the stage. The Monkeys at the sight of the nuts forgot their dancing and became (as indeed they were) Monkeys instead of actors. Pulling off their masks and tearing their robes, they fought with one another for the nuts. The dancing spectacle thus came to an end amidst the laughter and ridicule of the audience.*[269]

---

[269] *Aesop's Fables*, accessed Dec. 1, 2016, http://www.aesopfables.com/cgi/aesop1.cgi?sel&TheDancingMonkeys

A Courtier Bent on Mischief

As one who appreciates an honest and unwavering logical debate, yet values the role of a skeptic, allow me for this chapter, to play the part of one throwing a handful of macadamia nuts "upon the stage." Whether I play the role of skeptic or advocate, and to whom, I leave the reader to decide. I do, however, postulate the monkeys in the fable to be emblematic of naturalistic reasoning associated with the New Atheist's worldview. These humanistic theories are dressed up in fine clothes and cheerfully paraded around university campuses across the land. Not to be outdone by academia, many in the entertainment industry enjoy a continuous staging of presentations featuring the "dancing monkeys" as well. Naturalistic ideology is persistently embedded in more and more books, movies, articles, and television shows.[270] People of religious faith are concerned that the number of those who believe in God is in decline.

Tim Keller echoes this concern: "The non-churchgoing population in the United States and Europe is steadily increasing. The number of Americans answering 'no religious preference' to poll questions has skyrocketed, having doubled or even tripled in the last decade."[271] Nevertheless, Keller points out that churches and organizations with "supposedly obsolete beliefs in an infallible Bible and miracles are growing in the United States and exploding in Africa, Latin America, and Asia. Even in much of Europe, there is some growth in church attendance."[272] So this

---

[270] Timothy Keller, *The Reason for God* (New York, NY: Riverhead Books, 2008), ix.
[271] Ibid, x.
[272] Ibid, x.

raises the question of who is right. It appears both sides have what they believe to be a principled mindset to support their case. However, it is important to note that not all ideas are necessarily worthy or sound ideas. But rather, the paramount positions are openly discussed, thoroughly debated, and critically analyzed, including those that disagree with or are in alignment with theistic ideology and a biblical worldview.

Like a four-bladed propeller on a ship, four main philosophical arguments serve to drive belief in God forward. These arguments are not offered in an attempt to prove the claims of the Christian God *a priori*, but rather to establish the existence of God in general. It is important to remember; "Theistic proofs thus form part of Christian apologetics, but not the whole of it. Their aim is to establish rationally the existence – and certain core attributes of God. They do not fully fill out all of the attributes of the Christian God, nor all the Christian worldview."[273] These four cogent arguments help support the aforementioned thesis while building a foundational core toward an interrelated view of Christianity. So begins the first toss.

The First Nut

The Ontological Argument

The Ontological argument for God's existence "claims that proper reasoning about the idea of a Perfect Being generates

---

[273] Douglas Groothuis, *Christian Apologetics A Comprehensive Case for Biblical Faith* (Downers Grove, Il: InterVarsity Press, 2011), 172.

the conclusion that God exists."[274] This argument holds that God's existence is logical and necessarily holds true with zero reliance upon disputable empirical conditions. This argument is credited to St. Anselm (c. 1033-1109). In chapter three of *Proslogium,* Anselm writes, "God cannot be conceived not to exist. God is that, than which nothing greater can be conceived. That which can be conceived not to exist is not God."[275] From this thought, it follows that God is the type of being that possesses necessary existence, meaning "God exists as a matter of logical necessity. God does not exist as a contingent state of affairs."[276] As a necessary being, God would possess numerous qualities. Two that are often debated in an attempt to remove this nut from the stage are omniscience (all-knowingness) and omnipotence (all-powerfulness). Critics attack these two attributes in an effort to make the philosophical, and thereby logical, coherence of the Ontological argument "nonsensical or contradictory."[277]

God Can't Know All Things

In an attempt to knock out omniscience, critics claim, "since God is intrinsically without a body, God cannot possibly know what it feels like to have a body with its attendant pains and pleasures. Since God lacks knowledge, God cannot be omniscient."[278] Therefore, such critics reason that the idea of God contradicts itself. The mistake with this argument is a failure to

---

[274] Ibid, 185.
[275] Anselm, *Proslogium 3*, accessed Dec. 2, 2016, http://sourcebooks.fordham.edu/halsall/basis/anselm-proslogium.asp#CHAPTER%20III
[276] Groothuis, *Christian Apologetics A Comprehensive Case for Biblical Faith*, 195.
[277] Ibid, 195.
[278] Ibid, 196.

grasp the Christian concept of God. The Christian view of God does not claim that God has a personal "first-person *experience* of all that occurs in any sentient being in the universe, but that God has *knowledge* (justified true belief) of all propositions, both true and false."[279] Furthermore, Christianity teaches God took the form of a man. So, according to Christian doctrine, the second person of the Trinity took upon Himself flesh and blood through the incarnation (John 1:14; Philippians 2:5-8). Groothuis writes, "Therefore, God does know something of the embodied human condition in the first person. God knows what it is like to be a human."[280] We can then conclude that the critic's argument fails because God, in the Christian view, does have knowledge of all things including what it is like to be human.

Paradox of the Stone

A second attack on the Ontological argument is the famous "paradox of the stone" (POS) reasoning. The assertion examines the question of whether God can create a rock so heavy that he cannot move it, thereby concluding that if God is unable to create a stone too heavy to move, then he is not all-powerful since he is unable to create something. Moreover, if God cannot move a rock too heavy to move, then he is likewise not all-powerful since there is an object he cannot move. The critic contends this paradox proves omnipotence is illogical, and therefore God cannot exist. The problem with this paradox is a miscalculation between reason and all-powerfulness.

---

[279] Ibid, 196.
[280] Ibid, 197.

Aquinas answers this dilemma by saying, "God's power only pertains to actualizing logically possible states of affairs; it does not apply to actualizing logically impossible conditions. God cannot make a square circle."[281] To push the retort one step further, utilizing a modern-day example, NBC is unable to create a new reality TV show called The Married Bachelor. Why, because there is no such thing as a married bachelor. This POS argumentation fails because God cannot logically create conditions that contradict His omnipotence. Let us toss another nut onto the stage.

The Second Nut

The Cosmological Argument

The Cosmological Argument finds its potency in the concept of the universe owing its existence to something outside itself. This dependency on an outside source is found in both the creation of the universe and the sustaining force of its current existence. These concepts truly come to a tipping point with the question, "why is there something rather than nothing?" Philosophers across the ages (Kant, Russell, Leibniz, Heidegger, and Craig) have written widely concerning this question. It seems to me, the superior resolution is found within the Cosmological argument with its convincing logical conclusion of a first cause.

Who Created God

One of the common mistakes, however, is a misconstruction of the first premise. Some critics have altered the

---
[281] Ibid, 197.

first premise to, "Everything that exists must have a cause."[282] From this, the critic asks, since God exists, who created God? In fact, Bertrand Russell wrote of this classic straw man fallacy, "If everything must have a cause, then God must have a cause. If there can be anything without a cause, it may just as well be the world as God, so that there cannot be any validity in that argument."[283] The problem with Russell's assessment is, no actual Cosmological argument holds the premise that "everything must have a cause." Rather, God is the first cause as a self-sufficient and "factually necessary being; that is, God's original factuality is required to explain all the facts of the universe."[284] Therefore, the first premise is best summarized in the Kalam Cosmological Argument (KCA) developed in the Middle Ages.

Whatever Begins to Exist

The first premise of the KCA states, "Whatever begins to exist has a cause." From there, Craig points out, "The universe began to exist. Therefore, the universe has a cause and the cause of the universe is God."[285] It all begins with the first premise, "ex nihilo nihil fit" ('out of nothing, nothing comes').[286] If the critic wishes to argue otherwise, he needs to show clear and convincing proof, both philosophically and scientifically, that material matter can simply pop into existence from nothing. We can suppose this is a burden too large to bear upon sound logic and scientific

---

[282] Ibid, 209.
[283] Bertrand Russell, *Why I am not a Christian and Other Essays on Religion and Related Subjects*, ed. Paul Edwards (New York: Simon & Schuster, 1957), pp. 6-7.
[284] Groothuis, *Christian Apologetics A Comprehensive Case for Biblical Faith*, 210.
[285] Ibid, 214.
[286] Ibid, 215.

observation of how our universe works. It seems to me it is illogical at best, and irresponsible at least, to affirm, as Russell did, "The universe was 'just there' and in need of no explanation."[287] Although, if that is the course a critic wishes to take, even the Naturalist David Hume is waiting with a reply: "Allow me to tell you that I never asserted so absurd a Proposition as *that anything might arise without a cause*."[288] It is logical and coherent to conclude that nothing creates nothing and sustains nothing. Therefore, if the universe is a something, then something or someone is the cause.

The Universe is not Eternal

Lastly, we know from big bang cosmology that the universe is not eternal and had a beginning at a finite time ago. We also know that our universe is rapidly expanding and will cease to exist at a future date.[289] This knowledge leaves us with a stark contradiction between a Naturalistic worldview and a Theistic worldview. The former view ultimately degenerates into nihilism, while the latter view centers around hope. Groothuis concludes, "Unbelief in God as the originating cause of the universe results in a blind leap of faith in nothing at all at the source of everything whatsoever . . . Unless one posits that everything came from nothing without a cause, one must concede that a supernatural

---

[287] Ibid, 211.
[288] David Hume, *"To John Stewart," Letter 91*, ed. J.Y.T. Greig (Oxford, Eng: Clarendon, 1932), 1:187.
[289] William Lane Craig, *The Existence of God and the Beginning of the Universe*, accessed Dec. 1, 20016, http://www.reasonablefaith.org/the-existence-of-god-and-the-beginning-of-the-universe

Creator detonated the big bang."[290] Therefore, it is reasonable to conclude the KCA is of help in one's search for belief in God.

The Third Nut

The Moral Argument

The third nut tossed upon the stage is the Moral Argument (MA) for God's existence. In my opinion, this argument is by far the most humanly intuitive and easily accessible argument for us to understand. For example, moral outrage within the human experience is undoubtedly real and widely experienced. We often find ourselves making statements and giving direction to other people, utilizing words like *you ought, you should,* or *you must.* But where do we get this sense of commanding people they *ought, should,* or *must* do anything? Furthermore, where does this authority to command anyone or anything come from? Moreover, why do we experience a personal sense of outrage, offense, or anger when we hear of or see child abuse, social injustice, or genocide? Somehow, we conclude internally that there is something *just not right* about these situations and we have a *duty* to stop certain despicable deeds. It seems to me that this type of moral outrage and moral intuition points an arrow in the direction of objective moral values and duties. This, in turn, raises the question of where these objective values and duties come from. From a Theistic point of view, we hold that objective moral values are centered on the personhood and character of God; meaning,

---

[290] Groothuis, *Christian Apologetics A Comprehensive Case for Biblical Faith,* 232.

goodness is right because God is good and love is superior to hate because God is love. Simply put, God is the moral authority.

Why Naturalism Fails

Conversely, from a Naturalistic point of view, we have no right to conclude anything regarding an objective moral authority other than morality is personal, and we are unable to secure any type of higher moral authority than each individual's personal perspective. Determining morality from the individual perspective and way of thinking results in a relativistic worldview. Consequently, relativism ultimately leaves us with no true right or wrong concerning individual or corporate actions. Eventually, the moral debate erodes into a "Who Says" discussion. How do we ultimately know who or what is right or wrong? Is the ultimate decision-maker the individual, the majority, or some other subjective entity? Logically speaking, it does not matter whether we are asking this at the individual or societal level. In either case, who is to decide who or what is right? The answer, sadly, is no one. How can one culture say to another culture what is right or wrong?

Under Naturalism, there is simply no objective justification for moral reform or moral outrage. The work of Martin Luther King Jr., Mother Teresa, Harriet Tubman, Gandhi, and others, under Naturalism, is worthless and irrelevant. Issues of slavery, euthanasia, human medical experiments on the disabled, or other reprehensible actions cannot be objectively judged under this worldview. Naturalism pushes human sensibility to the brink.

For a worldview to be coherent, it must make sense of the world and the internal sensibilities of the human experience. Naturalism fails on this point.

Why Relativism Fails

Lastly, if we follow Relativism to its natural conclusion, meaning life without objective moral values, we end in Nihilism. German philosopher Max Stirner (1806-1856), echoing Nietzsche while a contemporary of Karl Marx wrote, "You think that the 'good cause' must be my concern? What's good, what's bad? Why, I myself am my concern, and I am neither good nor bad. Neither has meaning for me . . . Nothing is more to me than myself."[291] When pushed to its conclusion, Nihilism leaves us with no truth and no hope. We end in a life dedicated to self with no greater good but our desires. Groothuis concludes, "The concept of rights, whether found intrinsically in the person or conferred by the state, is a fiction. The concept of right is just another unreal absolute placed above the individual ego."[292] The Moral Argument provides additional support for God's existence because objective moral truth makes sense to us from an internal perspective. Objective moral laws must have a moral lawgiver.

The Fourth Nut

The Design Argument

As the fourth and final nut, the Design Argument (DA)

---

[291] Max Stirner, *The Ego and Its Own* (New York: NY, Libertarian Bk Club, 1963), 185.
[292] Groothuis, *Christian Apologetics A Comprehensive Case for Biblical Faith*, 344.

supports the view that our universe has been finely tuned for our existence. This argument raises the question, "if we see design, is there a designer?" From a Theistic perspective, we affirm, "that the universe is the handiwork of a designing agent. The Creator brought everything into existence *ex nihilo* and engineered the structure and function of the universe.[293] For example, if we were to compare the Grand Canyon to Mount Rushmore, it would be easy to conclude natural forces created the former while a designer created the latter. It is important also to note that the DA looks beyond random chance and apparent design in the universe.

In truth, there are wonders within our universe that appear designed, but under further inquiry, we discover natural laws plus time created the illusion of design. This has brought some to conclude along with "Choruses of secular voices, many of whom shout loudly from the scientific academy . . . that humans and the rest of the cosmos are nothing but the result of time, space, matter/energy, impersonal laws and chance."[294] However, this chorus of scientific and philosophical vocalists was challenged when "one of the twentieth century's leading atheist philosophers," Antony Flew "renounced atheism in 2007 on the basis of the evidence for a Designer and a Creator." Flew was clear in his bestselling book *There is a God* that he endeavored to "follow the argument where ever it leads."[295] As he followed the evidence for design, he landed upon the belief in a designer.

---

[293] Ibid, 344.
[294] Ibid, 240.
[295] Antony Flew with Ray Abraham Varghese, *There Is a God* (San Francisco, CA: HarperOne, 2007), 88.

Important Distinction

An important distinction must be made at this point. When applying the DA, I am using the argument in the sense of "the design inference" to remove other explanations.[296] This is not a new concept, nor is this an argument not fully utilized in other fields. In fact, empirical strategies for discovering intelligence are widely accepted in "several areas of archaeology, forensic science, intellectual property law, insurance claims investigation, [and] cryptography . . . Intelligent Design (ID) simply employs these methods of detecting or falsifying design and applies them to the natural sciences as well."[297] Dembski explains that through the use of an "explanatory filter that filters out chance and necessity and checks for the marks of contingency, complexity and specificity," we can have great confidence that an "event or cause may be reckoned the result of an intelligent cause – as opposed to a nonintelligent, material cause – if it exhibits all three of these factors."[298] Allow me to provide definitions of these factors.

Dembski elaborates that an object or event is ***contingent*** "if it cannot be explained by automatic processes." For instance, the metamorphosis of a caterpillar into a butterfly is beautifully wondrous, yet we know the process is natural, yet Christmas lights adorning the front of your neighbor's home are contingent upon someone doing the job. The natural laws of gravity assure the lights do not float away into air, yet a designer is responsible for

---

[296] William Demski, *The Design Inference: Eliminating Chance Through Small Probabilities* (New York, NY: Cambridge University Press, 1998). *His ideas are further developed in No Free Lunch* (Lanham, MA: Rowman & Littlefield, 2002).
[297] Groothuis, *Christian Apologetics A Comprehensive Case for Biblical Faith*, 244.
[298] Ibid, 244.

the actual display. **Complexity** is connected to probability. Simply put, if an event or object is incredibly complex, the likelihood or probability of random chance being the cause decreases exponentially. **Specificity** deals with an object or event exhibiting "a pattern independent of its mere improbability."[299] Groothuis explains specificity with the following illustration,

> *If you randomly throw a dart against the side of a barn from twenty feet away, the place where the dart lands would be improbable in the sense that it might have landed in any number of places. If you were to paint a bull's-eye around the dart and then remark on what an accurate dart thrower you were, this would be what Dembski identifies as a fabrication and not a specification. However, if a bull's-eye is painted on the barn before the dart is thrown and the thrower hits the bull's-eye, the result is specified. This likely indicates skill instead of luck – especially if the results are repeated. On the other hand, chance and necessity can adequately explain the destination of the randomly hurled dart.*[300]

Utilizing the design filter when looking for specified complexity in the natural world enhances the confidence in DA in concluding an intelligent source is inferred beyond the event or object.

God of the Gaps

Skeptics object to using design arguments all together, saying they amount to nothing more than a "God of the gaps" (GotG) ideology. Detractors of the DA claim GotG, as a logical

---
[299] Ibid, 245.
[300] Ibid, 245.

fallacy, is employed by Theists to fill in explanations instead of finding reasons behind our "ignorance of the natural world."[301] These critics point out that Isaac Newton "postulated divine causation to explain some of the gaps in his theories of planetary motion,"[302] but later, scientific evidence solved these theories with better data and further inquiry. This may be true in Newton's case; however, "this narrative is naïve and often begs the question in favor of naturalism."[303] Even though natural laws have been shown to provide answers to perplexing questions, it does not necessarily follow that supernatural explanation should be automatically ruled out, especially concerning the following elements of our fine-tuned universe. Consider the following observations.

The God of Design

Stephen Hawking's comments on the initial conditions of our universe that created a unique environment for us are significant: "If the rate of expansion one second after the big bang had been smaller by even one part in a hundred thousand million, million, the universe would have recollapsed . . . if the expansion rate at one second had been larger by the same amount, the universe would have expanded so much that it would be effectively empty now."[304] Physicist Roger Penrose discusses the unfathomable statistical probability required for us to be here: "How big was the original phase-volume . . . The Creator's aim

---

[301] Ibid, 246.
[302] Ibid, 246.
[303] Ibid, 247.
[304] Ibid, 250.

must have been [precise] to an accuracy of one part in $10^{10^{123}}$. One could not possibly write the number down . . . it would be 1 followed by 10^{123} successive '0's! [This is] the precision needed to set the universe on its course."[305] Astronomer Sir Martin Rees makes the observation that if the mathematics were off by "the tiniest degree, there would be no stars, no complex element, no life."[306] Robin Collins writes, "If the strength of gravity were changed by one part in ten thousand billion, billion, billion – relative to the 'total range of the strengths of the forces of nature (which span a range of 10 to the 40th)' – there would likely be no humanly populated world."[307]

Someone Monkeyed with the Physics

Fred Hoyle concluded, "A common sense interpretation of the facts suggests that a super intellect has monkeyed with the physics, as well as the chemistry and biology, and that there are no blind forces worth speaking about in nature"[308] Physicist Freeman Dyson wrote in his book *Disturbing the Universe*, "The more I examine the universe and study the details of its architecture, the more evidence I find that the universe in some sense must have known we were coming."[309]

Astrophysicist Hugh Ross observes, "The more thoroughly researchers investigate the history of our planet, the more astonishing the story of our existence becomes. The number

---

[305] Ibid, 250.
[306] Ibid, 251.
[307] Ibid, 252.
[308] Ibid, 253.
[309] Hugh Ross, *Improbable Planet* (Grand Rapids, MI: Baker Books, 2016), 42.

and complexity of the astronomical, geological, chemical, and biological features recognized as essential to human existence have expanded explosively within the past decade."[310]

Naturalism has no Answers

Naturalism has no answers for these inquiries and observations. To pronounce the Design Argument as nothing more than God of the Gaps reasoning is to hide from the reality of the unique intricacy of our universe and human existence. The fine-tuning of our universe and planet that enables human life to flourish can be attributed to a personal Creator or blind chance. Applying the above-mentioned design filter of **contingency**, **complexity**, and **specificity** is helpful in deciding between the two possibilities.

Contingency & Complexity - Check

It is reasonable to conclude, the design of universe is not contingent upon any known natural laws. Therefore, a designer cannot be ruled out, even though the universe does run and is supported by natural laws. Those natural laws, however, function no differently than the gravity holding the neighbors' Christmas lights in place. It appears to me, then, that the contingency test is passed. This box can be check in favor of a Creator. Secondly, it seems reasonable to conclude that our universe is unfathomably complex. In fact, frequent scientific discovery supports deeper and continual complexity in our universe. Groothuis writes, "The

---

[310] Ibid, 14.

greater the complexity, the less the probability that the event or object came about by chance – that is, without intelligent causation."[311] This box can be checked in favor of a Creator.

Specificity - Check

Lastly, since "contingency and complexity are necessary but not sufficient indicators of design,"[312] the specificity requirement must be met. Prior to answering the requirement, consider the following analogy from Groothuis. Suppose you flew to Mars, and when you arrived, you noticed a huge biosphere. In the facility was everything you and your party needed to survive and flourish. In the control room, you noticed a series of dials and levers that controlled all the necessary functions that made life for you possible on Mars; atmospheric buttons, biological measurements, plate tectonics controls, oxygenation quantities, and a myriad of other fine-tuned metrics that if off by .0000000000000000001% in any direction would mean certain death for you and your party. In other words, you noticed a very distinct bubble that was fine-tuned for your existence. Would it be reasonable to conclude that perhaps a designer designed this bubble? Of course, it would. In truth, for you to conclude it was by chance or natural law would be irrational. If we take the bubble of Mars and simply expand it out to include the bubble of our universe, it seems reasonable to conclude that our universe contains the specificity needed to check the box for a designer.

---

[311] Ibid, 245.
[312] Ibid, 245.

Concluding Thoughts

As the monkeys and trainers amicably exit the stage, with macadamia nuts firmly clenched within their hands, the dialogue regarding the truth claims of Biblical Christianity can begin. We have witnessed the persuasive rationality of the Ontological, Cosmological, Moral, and Design arguments methodically reveal the disadvantage of the case from disbelief. We still have some work to do in bringing one to the conclusion of Biblical Christianity being reasonable on its own merit. However, the philosophical groundwork accomplished within this chapter is notable for one to, at a minimum, start the journey toward uncovering the veracity of the Christian truth claims. Additional study is necessary to accomplish this goal, and throughout this volume, we have explored further avenues supporting the overall dynamic perspective of developing a personal faith in Jesus Christ. Further volumes will examine in greater detail the historical, archeological, and experiential case for Christianity, along with additional research on the scientific foundations relating to the origin of life discussions with a particular emphasis on DNA and biological wonders.

I began this chapter with the goal in mind of pointing to the conclusion that one who chooses to disbelieve in the existence of God does so for other reasons beyond having enough compelling evidence pointing to a conclusion that belief in God is logical. The Ontological argument shows that God is the type of being that possesses necessary existence. The Cosmological argument reveals the universe owing its existence to something outside itself. The Moral argument holds that objective moral laws do exist and objective moral laws must have a moral lawgiver. The Design argument shows that our universe has been finely tuned for our existence. The evidence has been thoroughly revealed, the logic is sound, and the detractors have exited the stage. All that remains is for each audience member to draw his or her own conclusion as to the effectiveness of this case.

CHAPTER TEN
The Problem of Evil

The Overview

In Christopher Browning's 1992 book entitled, *Ordinary Men*, he details a number of disturbing accounts regarding the Holocaust of World War II. The extermination of six million European Jews including one and half million children[313] at the hands of Adolf Hitler's Nazi Germany is an unconscionable reminder of the sheer barbarism and depravity of humankind. Browning's book tells the story of the unsettling reality regarding a Reserve Police Battalion, composed of ordinary men, who ultimately turned into a killing machine for their country. The amount of evil revealed within the pages of his book leaves the reader very uncomfortable, to say the least, but leaves no doubt that evil is real, on an individual and a group level.

---

[313] http://magazine.foi.org/inside-yad-vashem, accessed, May 08, 2017

As gruesome as this account is, regrettably, history is filled with further evils perpetrated upon other people groups throughout the world. A natural question to ask when we see and hear of these events is if God exists, then why does He allow this type of evil and suffering? Perhaps we should take this line of questioning one step further, why does God allow any type of evil or suffering at all? Prior to answering the why question, critics of theism hold that the existence of evil is contradictory to the existence of God. In other words, if God is all-powerful, all-knowing, and all-loving, evil cannot exist. But, the critic says, since we see evil all around us, therefore God does not exist. Even though critics of theism believe the problem of evil to be a defeater concerning the existence of God, I will argue the free will defense is adequate in showing how the existence of God and evil are compatible.

Defining The Problem of Evil

It is important to note there are two subsections regarding the problem of evil. John Feinberg comments, "There is initially a distinction between what I shall call the religious problem of evil and the theological/philosophical problem of evil." [314] He continues in describing how the religious problem of evil can arise when a person is faced with a personal affliction or witnesses a human tragedy. The person then begins to wonder how God could allow this to happen. For many, Feinberg points out, "This

---

[314] John S. Feinberg, *The Many Faces of Evil* (Wheaton, IL; Crossway, 2004), 21.

precipitates a crisis of faith"³¹⁵ and a searching for spiritual answers ensues. The biblical example of Job comes to mind when thinking of this distinction. Unfortunately, the length of this chapter will not afford the opportunity for me to address the religious problem of evil adequately. Suffice to say, at this point, unless the logical problem of evil is settled first, a solution to the religious problem of evil is of little consequence.

While the religious problem of evil deals with our gut reaction or feelings on the topic of evil, "the theological/philosophical problem of evil is about the existence of evil in general, not some specific evil that someone encounters which disrupts her personal relation with God."³¹⁶ In fact, Fienberg points out, the theological/philosophical problem of evil is disconnected from the experiential evil we see and feel every day. Some call this the logical problem of evil, as the concern is an intellectual contradiction in the idea of an all-knowing, all-powerful, and all-benevolent God who allows His creatures to suffer moral and natural evils.

A Contradiction

Those who hold to an atheistic worldview charge theists with committing intellectual dishonesty by holding to a view that God and evil exist. The atheist claims a morally perfect God could not possibly allow evil to exist because it would be morally challenging for him, and would stand in opposition to his nature.

---

³¹⁵ Ibid, 21.
³¹⁶ Ibid, 21.

In referring to the logical problem of evil, J.L. Mackie writes, "Here it can be shown, not that religious beliefs lack rational support, but that they are positively irrational, that several parts of the essential theological doctrine are inconsistent with one another."[317]

Additional support for Mackie's view comes from H.J. McCloskey, "Evil is a problem, for the theist, in that a contradiction is involved in the fact of evil on the one hand and belief in the omnipotence and omniscience of God on the other."[318] Along with support from philosopher Antony Flew, these mid-twentieth century thinkers posed a significant problem for theists. They claim the following statements cannot be true at the same time.[319]

(1) God is omnipotent (that is, all-powerful)
(2) God is omniscient (that is, all-knowing)
(3) God is perfectly good
(4) Evil exists

The idea here is that the set of all four propositions exist in a logical contradiction. In other words, if God were all-powerful, He would be able to prevent all evil and suffering in the world. If God is all-knowing, He would be aware of all evil and would

---

[317] Mackie, J.L. 1955. Evil and Omnipotence *Mind* 64:200-212. http://www.douglasficek.com/teaching/phil-2250/evil-and-omnipotence.pdf, accessed, May 4, 2017.
[318] McCloskey, H.J. 1960. "God and Evil" *Philosophical Quarterly* 10: 97-114.
[319] http://www.iep.utm.edu/evil-log, accessed, May 2, 2017

know how to prevent or stop it. Finally, if God were all-loving and perfectly good, He would want to block all evil and anguish on the earth.[320] But since evil does exist and God does not prevent evil from happening, He must not be omnipotent, omniscient, or perfectly good, or so the argument goes. To summarize their argument,

> (5) If evil and suffering exist, then God is either not omnipotent, not omniscient, or not perfectly good
> ***Since evil and suffering do exist from (4) above***
> (6) God is either not omnipotent, not omniscient, or not perfectly good.

The Missing Step

Yet the theist holds that (1) through (3) are true and confirm the existence of evil (4) as well. Apparently, the theist is performing some type of mental gymnastics unless Mackie, McCloskey, and Flew are missing a critical logical step in their argument. Alister McGrath points out what is missing, "At least one further premise must be added to this list if a logical inconsistency is to result,

> (7) A good and omnipotent God could eliminate suffering [evil] entirely
> (8) There could not be morally sufficient reasons for God permitting suffering [evil]

---

[320] Ibid.

If either of these propositions could be shown to be correct, a major and potentially fatal flaw in the Christian conception of God would have been exposed."[321] Meaning, if God has a morally sufficient reason for allowing evil to exist and, by virtue of our human nature, evil necessarily exists, the theist has a strong defense versus the logical problem of evil.

Free Will Defense

Philosopher Alvin Plantinga, in the 1970's, offered an influential answer for God having a morally sufficient reason for allowing evil to exist with the Free Will Defense. This is not a new defense to the problem evil; in fact, Augustine utilized a similar form in his day. Additionally, many theologians throughout history have employed the same defense. However, Plantinga advanced the argument by pointing out, "God's creation of persons with morally significant free will is something of tremendous value. God could not eliminate much of the evil and suffering in this world without thereby eliminating the greater good of having created persons with free will with whom he could have relationships and who are able to love one another and do good deeds."[322] Plantinga's argument basically says God can have a morally sufficient reason for allowing evil to exist in order to

---

[321] Alister E. McGrath, *Intellectuals Don't Need God* (Grand Rapids, MI; Zondervan, 1992), 102.
[322] Plantinga, Alvin. 1974. *The Nature of Necessary*. Oxford: Oxford University Press. & 1977. *God, Freedom, and Evil*. Grand Rapids, MI: Eerdmans. http://www.iep.utm.edu/evil-log/ accessed, May 11, 2017.

reveal a greater good and if God removed evil, He would then have to remove the good.

A Good & Loving Parent

Perhaps an illustration can be of assistance; imagine you have a son who is critically allergic to nuts, and for some unfortunate reason, your child ingests food that contains nuts. Within minutes, you witness his breathing shorten, his airways tighten, and yet you are hours from any sort of medical facility. However, in your possession is an EpiPen containing the medicine able to reverse the effects of the allergic reaction. You know the injection of epinephrine through a needle will cause pain to your son's leg; however, the greater good of reversing the deadly reaction is a morally significant reason to cause momentary pain. Without hesitation, you immediately stick the needle into your son's leg, and his breathing returns to normal. As a good and loving parent, possessing both the knowledge and power to change the situation, you chose to allow pain even though you could have prevented it.

Humans are not Robots

Now, when Plantinga mentions "morally significant free will," what exactly does he mean? Plantinga holds to a libertarian view that is best defined as, "the view that a person is free with respect to a given action if and only if that person is both free to perform that action and free to refrain from performing that action; in other words, that person is not determined to perform or refrain from that action by any prior causal forces."³²³ This view holds that determinism is false and that God did not create human beings to be robots beholden to prior causes or a type of divine simulation platform. This is an important distinction when attempting to solve the problem of evil. Why, because if determinism is true, then God is the creator of evil. In fact, Clay Jones points out this uncomfortable conclusion by writing,

> If determinism is true—and God has determined every creature's every thought and deed so that they could never do otherwise—then the man who fantasized about how he would rape and torture to death the little girl next door, and then actually carried out his wicked scheme, was not able to do otherwise. This means that every exquisite torture, every penetration, burn, cut, crush, *ad infinitum, ad nauseam*, was indeed efficaciously arranged by God so that this torturer could not have done other than he did.³²⁴

Truthfully, determinism is such a difficult position to take for the Christian that even respected scholar and author R.C. Sproul, who holds a deterministic worldview admits, "I do not know the solution to the problem of evil. Nor do I know of anyone who does."³²⁵ Jones additionally points out, "even J.I. Packer when faced with explaining how God can determine absolutely everything and yet not be the author of evil makes a similar appeal but calls it an antinomy."³²⁶ Packer then continues to explain an

---

³²³ http://www.iep.utm.edu/evil-log, accessed, May 13, 2017.
³²⁴ Clay Jones, *Is Determinism Scriptural?* (La Mirada, CA; Biola University CSAP 628MD, 2017), 6.
³²⁵ R.C. Sproul, *The Invisible Hand: Do all Things Really Work for Good?* (Dallas, TX; Word, 1996), 167, as quoted in Clay Jones, *Is Determinism Scriptural?* (La Mirada, CA; Biola University CSAP 628MD, 2017), 6.
³²⁶ Ibid, 6.

antinomy, in theology, is a mystery of two apparent truths that we are unable to square together logically.

A Big Risk

It seems to me, this is a risky sort of conclusion because it causes uncertainty in deciding, "when a contradiction between two theologies is only an apparent contradiction and not a real contradiction."[327] The danger rests, according to Jones, in the cultist or otherwise simply claiming the same sort of thing when his theologies collide with logic. This is such a slippery slope theologically, that even determinist Paul Helm concludes that, "appealing to an antinomy could be a license for accepting nonsense."[328] The bigger issue here is determinism provides no solution to the logical problem of evil. In order to solve the problem, we say that God gives humanity free will, meaning "the ability to decide between alternatives."[329]

A World Without Evil

Libertarian free will is considered a "morally significant kind of free will"[330] according to Plantinga. We know an action is morally significant if we can evaluate the action against the backdrop of moral approval or fault. Some ask, why doesn't God create a world without pain and suffering, can He not create a world without evil? One could suppose that God has the ability

---

[327] Ibid, 6.
[328] Paul Helm, *The Providence of God: Contours of Christian Theology* (Downers Grove, IL; InterVarsity, 1993), 66.
[329] Norman L. Geisler, *When Skeptics Ask* (Grand Rapids, MI; Baker Books, 1990), 63.
[330] Ibid, accessed, May 13, 2017.

and power to create a world without evil, but according to Plantinga that world would be such that humans do not possess the capacity to perform morally significant actions. In other words, there would be no reason to praise good behavior or actions because the person had no option but to choose the right thing to do.

This again amounts to being programmed to do the right thing and is not the type of libertarian free will that we seem to know and understand as free moral agents. Some argue that if God is not able to create a world of free creatures in which those free creatures always chose the right thing to do shows that God is limited in His power and therefore does not possess the omnipotence the theist claims. C.S. Lewis tackles this very objection in his admired book *the Problem of Pain*. In it, he writes,

> If you chose to say "God can give a creature free-will and at the same time withhold free-will from it," you have not succeeded in saying *anything* about God: meaningless combination of words do not suddenly acquire a meaning because we prefix to them the two other words: "God can." It remains true that all *things* are possible with God: the intrinsic impossibilities are not things but nonentities. It is no more possible for God than for the weakest of his creatures to carry out both of two mutually exclusive alternatives, not because his power meets an obstacle, but because nonsense remains nonsense, even when we talk it about God.[331]

---

[331] C.S. Lewis, *The Problem of Pain*, as quoted in Alister E. McGrath, *Intellectuals Don't Need God* (Grand Rapids, MI; Zondervan, 1992), 103.

Consequently, we can conclude that God does not lack omnipotence as the non-theist claims. In truth, there are many things God is not able to do, yet we do not find He lacks power or an inability in some form. Consider the following,

- God is not able to lie
- God is not able to cheat
- God is not able to steal
- God is not able to be unjust
- God is not able to be envious
- God is not able to fail to know what is right
- God is not able to cease to exist[332]

On account of this list, it would be illogical to demand that God lacks omnipotence because He is not able to contradict His own character or nature. That would be like saying a married bachelor lacks the ability to get divorced. We understand this statement to be nonsensical because the inability to gain a divorce is not due to an incapability to perform a particular function but rather due to the nature of bachelor's not being married. To finalize his case, Plantinga adds two more to the *God is not able to* list,

> (9) God is not able to contradict Himself
>
> (10) God is not able to make significantly free creatures and to causally determine that they will always choose what is right and avoid what is wrong.

---

[332] http://www.iep.utm.edu/evil-log, accessed, May 13, 2017.

Therefore, the theist is logical in thinking that in a libertarian free will creation, God is not able to simply remove evil or control the actions of free agents who have the nature of choosing different alternatives whether good or bad. For God to restrict those decisions would be a contradiction of His created order.

What About Natural Evil

At this point, one could argue that Plantinga has solved the logical problem of moral evil. However, what about the problem of natural evil? When we say natural evil, we mean events like tornadoes, earthquakes, fire, and floods, or states of affairs like mental disorders, deformities, famines, or disease. It is logical to agree with the principle of free moral agents bearing the responsibility in a libertarian creation, thereby eventually being responsible for the moral evil we see and know. But how does God not bear the responsibility for natural evil like those listed above?

It seems entirely logical that God would do no harm by modifying or intruding upon our free will by choosing tomorrow to end all deaths from HIV or other deadly viruses. For that matter, why keep cancer around, should not God stop it tomorrow? If indeed the theist holds that all men die and then the judgment (Hebrews 9:27), cannot God find other less painful ways to bring us to the end of our earthly existence without impeding on our free will? Indeed with His all-knowing and all-loving nature, God could figure out a way to lessen the suffering or minimize the natural evil we experience, the critic requests. To be sure, this is not an audacious request. The theist would be in agreement on this point.

It is important to know, however, this line of thinking begins the dialogue into the religious problem of evil. It is here that we start the discussion and defense of *why* from an emotional or heartfelt level. Whereas this is certainly a very human thing to do, we must stay focused, in this chapter, on the intellectual solution first.

Plantinga's defense for the natural problem of evil is formulated by "holding that it is possible that all natural evil (destructive floods and earthquakes, for example) is really moral evil, because it is possible that it is evil resulting from the free actions of non-human agents, namely, Satan and his minions."[333] Critics and philosophers may object to this line of reasoning based upon improbability; however, for Plantinga to defeat Mackie, McCloskey, and Flew philosophically, he only needs to prove possibility and not probability.

Of interest to this discussion, Professor James R. Beebe shows an alternative justification for the natural problem of evil in that, "God allowed natural evil to enter the world as a part of Adam and Eve's punishment for their sin in the Garden of

---

[333] Dean-Peter Baker (ed.), *Alvin Plantinga*, Cambridge University Press, 2007, 233pp., http://ndpr.nd.edu/news/alvin-plantinga, accessed May 14, 2017.

Eden."[334] Again, the non-theist may not agree with either view from a personal, religious, or emotional point of view, but concerning a morally sufficient reason for God allowing natural evil to exist, either perspective supports the Free Will Defense.

Is The Problem Solved

In conclusion, Plantinga's case dispensed a deathblow to the logical problem of evil. In fact, in 1982, J.L. Mackie an outspoken supporter of the logical problem of evil and well-known atheist philosopher wrote the following regarding Plantinga's argument,

> *Since this defense is formally [that is, logically] possible, and its principle involves no real abandonment of our ordinary view of the opposition between good and evil, we can concede that the problem of evil does not, after all, show that the central doctrines of theism are logically inconsistent with one another. But whether this offers a real solution to the problem is another question.*[335]

We find that Plantinga's Free Will Defense succeeds in providing a logical possibility regarding the co-existence of God and evil. Keep in mind that Plantinga does not need to show or prove the actual reason for God allowing evil to exist, he just needs to show a possible reason why the two premises below are not correct,

> (7) A good and omnipotent God could eliminate suffering [evil] entirely

---

[334] http://www.iep.utm.edu/evil-log, accessed, May 13, 2017.
[335] Mackie, J.L. *The Miracle of Theism* (Oxford, Eng; Oxford University Press, 1982), 154.

(8) There could not be morally sufficient reasons for God permitting suffering [evil]

He accomplishes the task with the following two premises,

(9) God is not able to contradict Himself
(10) God is not able to make significantly free creatures and to causally determine that they will always choose what is right and avoid what is wrong.

Therefore, (5) and (6) fail,

(5) If evil and suffering exist, then God is either not omnipotent, not omniscient, or not perfectly good
(6) God is either not omnipotent, not omniscient, or not perfectly good

These propositions directed skeptics like Mackie, McCloskey, and Flew to conclude the set of (1) through (4) can exist in a logical form,

(1) God is omnipotent (that is, all-powerful)
(2) God is omniscient (that is, all-knowing)
(3) God is perfectly good
(4) Evil exists

With the logical problem of evil solved, the theist is well positioned to move on to the religious problem of evil. The religious problem of evil deals with the emotional side of the debate and is a very human response to desire an answer, as Job did, to why God allows us to experience pain and suffering in this world. C.S. Lewis gives a small hint as to God's motivation by writing, "God whispers to us in our pleasures, speaks in our conscience, but shouts in our pains: it is His megaphone to rouse a deaf world."[336] If indeed, God desires to have a loving relationship with His creatures, perhaps the best and in some cases the only way may be through suffering. If so, we can then understand Paul's words in 2 Corinthians 1:3-4, "Blessed be the God and Father of our Lord Jesus Christ, the Father of mercies and God of all comfort, who comforts us in all our affliction, so that we may be able to comfort those who are in any affliction, with the comfort with which we ourselves are comforted by God."

---

[336] C.S. Lewis, *The Problem of Pain* (New York, NY; Macmillan, 1962), 93.

T.K. Anderson

About the Author

Having served in pastoral ministry positions for 17 years and having served at the executive level of two Fortune 500 companies for 14 years, T.K. Anderson is a seasoned leader in both the affairs of business and Christian ministries.

He is the author of two books, ***Pocket Theology: Getting God*** and ***Faith Jump Vol. 1.0***, has spoken to tens of thousands of people in numerous countries around the globe, earned a Bachelor's degree in Theological Studies from North Central University and a Master's degree in Christian Apologetics from Biola University.

He is the founder of Faithjump.com and currently serves as Pastor of The Social Media Church (TSMchurch.com), and President of the National Institute of Apologetics.

T.K. Anderson

Bibliography

- Allison, Dale, *Resurrecting Jesus* (New York, NY: T&T Clark, 2005)
- Arnold, Clinton E., and David W.J. Gill, *Zondervan Illustrated Bible Backgrounds Commentary Volume 3* (Grand Rapids, MI; Zondervan, 2002)
- Aune, D.E., *Greco-Roman Literature and the New Testament: Selected Forms and Genres* (Atlanta, GA: Scholars Press, 1998)
- Baker, Dean-Peter, *Alvin Plantinga* (Cambridge University Press: 2007)
- Baylis, Albert H., *From Creation to the Cross* (Grand Rapids, MI: Zondervan, 1996)
- Brundage, James A., *The Crusades: A Documentary Survey* (Milwaukee, WI: Marquette University Press, 1962)
- Carson, D.A., *From Sabbath to Lord's Day* (Eugene, OR: Wipf and Stock Publishers, 1999)
- Craig, W.L. *Reasonable Faith: Christian Truth and Apologetics, Third Ed.* (Wheaton, IL: Crossway, 2008)
- Craig, W.L. Seminar, *The Historical Jesus & The Resurrection* (Atlanta, GA: April 7-8, 2017)
- Crawford, Paul, *Four Myths about the Crusades*, (accessed December 4, 2015)
- Crossan, John Dominic, *Jesus: A Revolutionary Biography*. (New York, NY: HarperOne 1995)

- Demski, William, *The Design Inference: Eliminating Chance Through Small Probabilities* (New York, NY: Cambridge University Press, 1998) & *No Free Lunch* (Lanham, MA: Rowman & Littlefield, 2002)
- Doherty, Earl, *Jesus: Neither God Nor Man.* (Ottawa, Canada: Age of Reason, 2009)
- Ehrman, Bart, *From Jesus to Constantine: A History of Early Christianity, Lecture 4: Oral and Written Traditions about Jesus* (The Teaching Company, 2003)
- Ehrman, Bart, *Did Jesus Exist* (New York, NY: Harper Collins, 2012)
- Evans, Craig A, *Jewish Burial Traditions and the Resurrection of Jesus.* (Thousand Oaks, CA: Journal for the Study of the Historical Jesus Vol. 3.2, SAGE Publications, 2005)
- Feinberg, John S., *The Many Faces of Evil* (Wheaton, IL: Crossway, 2004)
- Foreman, Mark W., *Come Let Us Reason.* (Nashville, TN: B&H Publishing Group, 2012)
- France, Richard T., *The Gospel of Mark* New International Greek Text Commentary (Grand Rapids, MI: Eerdmans, 2002)
- Fuller, R. H., *The Formation of the Resurrection Narratives* (London, Eng: SPCK, 1972)
- Geisler, Norman L. and Meister, Chad V. *Reasons for Faith: Making a Case for the Christian Faith* (Wheaton, IL: Crossway Books, 2007)

- Geisler, Norman L., & Ron Brooks, *When Skeptics Ask* (Wheaton, IL: Victor, 1990)
- Gilderhus, M.T., *History and Historians: A Historiographical Introduction* 6th ed. (Upper Saddle River, N.J: Prentice Hall, 2007)
- Gould, Paul, *The Problem of God and Abstract Objects: A Prolegomenon* (Philosophia Christi 13, 2011)
- Groothuis, Douglas, *Christian Apologetics A Comprehensive Case for Biblical Faith* (Downers Grove, Il: InterVarsity Press, 2011)
- Gundry, Stanley N., *Five Views on Law and Gospel* (Grand Rapids, MI: Zondervan, 1999)
- Habermas, Gary R., *Resurrection Research from 1975 to the Present* (Thousand Oaks, CA: Journal for the Study of the Historical Jesus, Vol. 3.2, SAGE Publications, 2005)
- Habermas, Gary R., "Explaining Away Jesus' Resurrection." *Explaining Away Jesus' Resurrection.* (Christian Research Journal, 2001. Web. 08 Sept. 2014)
- Helm, Paul, *The Providence of God: Contours of Christian Theology* (Downers Grove, IL: InterVarsity, 1993)
- Hitchens, Christopher, ed., *The Portable Atheist: Essential Readings for the Nonbeliever* (Philadelphia: Da Capo, 2007)
- Hollister, Warren, J. Sears McGee, and Gale Stokes, *The West Transformed: A History of Western Civilization, vol. 1* (New York: Cengage/Wadsworth, 2000)
- Hume, David, *"To John Stewart," Letter 91*, ed. J.Y.T. Greig (Oxford, Eng; Clarendon, 1932)

- Hurtado, Larry W., *Jesus' Resurrection in the Early Christian Texts* (Thousand Oaks, CA: Journal of the Study of the Historical Jesus, Vol. 3.2, SAGE Publications, 2005)
- Jones, Clay, *Is Determinism Scriptural* (La Mirada, CA: Biola University CSAP 628MD, 2017)
- Keener, Craig S., *The Historical Jesus of the Gospels* (Grand Rapids, MI: Eerdmans, 2009)
- Keller, Timothy, *The Reason for God* (New York, NY: Riverhead Books, 2008)
- Koester, Helmut, *Ancient Christian Gospels: Their History and Development.* (London, Eng: SCM, 1990)
- Lewis, C.S., *Letters of C.S. Lewis.* (New York, NY: Harcourt Brace, 1988)
- Lewis, C.S., *The Problem of Pain* (New York, NY: Macmillan, 1962)
- Lewis, C.S., *Surprised by Joy.* (New York, NY: Harcourt Brace, 1988)
- Lewis, C.S. Lewis, *Weight of Glory* (New York, NY: HarperOne, 1949)
- Licona, Michael R., *The Resurrection of Jesus* (Nottingham, Eng: IVP Academic, 2010)
- Lindsley, Art, *C.S. Lewis's Case For Christ.* (Downers Grove, IL: IVP Books, 2005)
- Lüdemann, Gerd, *What Really Happened to Jesus?* (Louisville, KY: Westminster John Knox Press, 1995)
- Mackie, J.L., *The Miracle of Theism* (Oxford, Eng; Oxford University Press, 1982)

- Maier, P.L., *Josephus: The Essential Works* (Grand Rapids: Kregel, 1994)
- Markos, Louis A., *Myth Matters Why C.S. Lewis's books remain models for Christian apologists in the 21st century* (Christianity Today The Magazine, April 23, 2001)
- McCloskey, H.J. 1960, "God and Evil" (*Philosophical Quarterly* 10: 97-114)
- McDowell, Josh, *The New Evidence that Demands a Verdict* (Nashville: Thomas Nelson, 1999)
- McGrath, Alister E., *Intellectuals Don't Need God.* (Grand Rapids, MI: Zondervan, 1992)
- Meier, John P., *A Marginal Jew: Rethinking the Historical Jesus* Vol. 2. (New York, NY: Doubleday, 1994)
- Meier, John P., *Tacitus Annuals.* 15.44 (English translations 1991)
- Moreland, J.P. & William Lane Craig, *Philosophical Foundations for a Christian Worldview* (Downers Grove, Il: InterVarsity Press, 2003)
- Newberg, Andrew, *Born To Believe* (New York, NY: Free Press, 2006)
- Noll, Mark A., *Turning Points Third Edition* (Grand Rapids, MI: Baker Academic, 2012)
- Patterson, Stephen J., *The God of Jesus: The Historical Jesus and the Search for Meaning* (Harrisburg, PA: Trinity Press International, 1998)
- Peoples, R. Scott, *Crusade of Kings* (Rockville, MD: Wildside, 2009)

- Perrin, Norman, *The Resurrection According to Matthew, Mark, and Luke* (Philadelphia, PA: Fortress, 1974)
- Plantinga, Alvin, *The Nature of Necessary* (Oxford: Oxford University Press, 1970) & *God, Freedom, and Evil* (Grand Rapids, MI: Eerdmans, 1977)
- Riley-Smith, Jonathan, *What Were the Crusades* (San Francisco, CA: Ignatius Press, 2009)
- Robinson, John A. T., *The Human Face of God* (Philadelphia, PA: Westminster, 1973)
- Ross, Hugh, *Improbable Planet* (Grand Rapids, MI: Baker Books, 2016)
- Runciman, Sir Steven, *A History of the Crusades: Vol. III, The Kingdom of Acre and the Later Crusades* (Cambridge: Cambridge University Press, 1954)
- Russell, Bertrand, *Why I am not a Christian and Other Essays on Religion and Related Subjects*, ed. Paul Edwards (New York: Simon & Schuster, 1957)
- Shelley, Bruce L., *Church History In Plain Language 4th ed.* (Nashville, TN: Thomas Nelson, 2013)
- Smith, R. Scott, *Craig's Nominalism and the High Cost of Preserving Divine Aseity* (Biola University, CSSR 660 MD1 SpTpcs: Coherence of Theism, 2014)
- Smith R. Scott, *William Lane Craig's Nominalism, Essences, and Implications for Our knowledge of Reality* (Philosophia Christi Vol. 15, No. 2, 2013)
- Sproul, R.C., *The Invisible Hand: Do all Things Really Work for Good* (Dallas, TX: Word, 1996)

- Stark, Rodney, *God's Battalions* (New York, NY: HarperOne, 2009)
- Stenger, Victor J., *God: The Failed Hypothesis–How Science Shows That God Does Not Exist* (Amherst, NY: Prometheus, 2008)
- Stirner, Max, *The Ego and Its Own* (New York: NY, Libertarian Book Club, 1963)
- Stokes, Mitch, *How to be an atheist: Why Skeptics Aren't Skeptical Enough* (Wheaton, Il: Crossway, 2016)
- Strobel, Lee, *The Case for Christ: A Journalist's Personal Investigation of the Evidence for Jesus* (Grand Rapids, MI: Zondervan, 1998)
- Strobel, Lee, *The Case For The Real Jesus.* (New York, NY: Zondervan, 2007)
- Theissen and Winter, *Quest for the Plausible Jesus* (Edinburgh, Scotland: T&T Clark, 1906; 3rd ed, 1911)
- Tolkien, J.R.R., ltr 31 in *The Letters of J.R.R. Tolkien* (New York, NY: Houghton Mifflin, 1981)
- Varney, Allen, *The Crusades: Campaign Sourcebook, ed.* (Lake Geneva, WI: TSR, 1994)
- Wineland, John E., ed., *The Light of Discovery.* (Eugene, OR: Pickwick, 2007)
- Wright, N.T., *The Resurrection of the Son of God* (Minneapolis, MN: Fortress Press, 2003)

www.ingramcontent.com/pod-product-compliance
Lightning Source LLC
Chambersburg PA
CBHW061644040426
42446CB00010B/1565